CUSTOMIZED VERSION OF

LEARNING TO DANCE

DANCE AS AN ART FORM AND ENTERTAINMENT

Designed Specifically for Kitty Sutton

at University of South Carolina

KENDALL/HUNT PUBLISHING COMPANY
4050 Westmark Drive   Dubuque, Iowa 52002

C O N T E N T S

INTRODUCTION

THE THEATER

Dance can be seen in many venues. It may be performed in the streets, in a park on an outdoor stage, in a classroom or studio, in a gymnasium, or in any number of settings. Often, though, dance is viewed by an audience in a theater setting. One type of stage is called "theater in the round," in which the stage is located in the center with the audience seated surrounding the stage. The more usual stage is called the "**proscenium stage**," in which the audience is seated in front of the stage, separating the audience from the performers. The **proscenium arch** separates the stage from the auditorium.

It is important to understand some stage terminology. The focal point of the stage is in the middle and is called "**center stage**." From the dancer's point of view, the area to the right is "**stage right**," and to his or her left is called "**stage left**," although this may seem to be "backwards" from the audience's perspective. The forward part of the stage (towards the audience) is "**downstage**," and to the rear of center is "**upstage**." On either side of the stage are the "**wings**," where the dancers wait off stage to make their entrance and make their exits. A **cyclorama** or "cyc" is a type of backdrop or curtain hung in the upstage area which was originally used to give the illusion of motion, but which today can be made to take on different colors by the use of lighting. A **scrim** is an open weaved fabric or curtain which, under certain lighting conditions, creates the illusion of a solid wall or background, but which when lit from behind becomes semitransparent, allowing the audience to see through it to the action behind it.

OBSERVING DANCE

There are many genres or types of dance which can be performed in the theater. We may see a classical ballet, a contemporary piece, hip hop, or musical theater being performed, just to name a few. But there are some common elements which can be observed among these genres which help in the understanding of the performance. Some elements for consideration are:

CHOREOGRAPHY

Choreography is the art of composing dances and planning and arranging the movements, steps and patterns of the dancers. The **choreographer** is the person who plans and creates the movements. In discussing the choreography, you will want to observe several things. What style or genre of dance is being performed? The audience should have certain expectations when observing, for example, a classical ballet, which would be quite different from what might be seen in a tap dancing performance. What is the choreographer trying to accomplish? Is he or she telling a story, or is the dance simply abstract, with no story line? What patterns may be observed? Perhaps the choreographer will use big, large broad movement, with many turns or jumps. Or perhaps he or she will have the dancers remain more grounded, perhaps even lying on the stage. Is the entire stage used, with movements to both stage left and right, and both upstage and downstage? Or do the dancers remain somewhat stationary, with little movement across the stage?

THE DANCERS

Observe the performance of the dancers themselves. Are they professionals, amateurs, or student performers? Are they rehearsed and prepared for the performance? Are they cast appropriately for the role they are dancing? Look at the number of dancers on stage. Are there solo performers? Do they perform as a duo, or a pas de deux (step of two)? Are there both male and female dancers, and how do they interact?

THE LIGHTING

The lighting for each dance is planned just as the dance steps themselves are. A **lighting director** works with the choreographer to create the vision that the choreographer has in mind. Look at the colors of lighting that have been selected. "Warm" tones, such as yellows or reds might set one mood, while "cool" tones such as greens or blues set another. Lights are placed in the front and over the stage, and also from behind. Further, they are placed in the wings so that all sides of the dancer may be lit.

SET/SCENERY

A backdrop may be painted to set a scene for a ballet. For example, in the classical ballet "The Nutcracker," usually an elaborate set is used to show that the ballet is taking place at Christmas. Scenery and "props" might be used to further the action. For example, a Christmas tree is a prop, as is the nutcracker itself. Other times, a conscious decision might be made to use absolutely no set or scenery. The famous choreographer George Balanchine intentionally used no set in many of his ballets, making the dancers themselves the focus and keeping a "clean" stage.

COSTUMES/MAKE UP

A **costume designer** and **make up artist** work with the choreographer to achieve the artistic vision. What type of costume is used? It might be a simple leotard, or in the case of Modern dance, a unitard. Or it could be a classical tutu for the females and a tunic and tights for the male dancers. What colors and fabrics were selected? Is elaborate make-up used, or simple stage make-up for the dancers?

MUSIC

The music for each genre of dance may be very different. Is the music recorded, or is it being performed by live musicians or an orchestra? Is the music classical, or is it more discordant, or even computer generated? Consider how the music works with the choreography.

THEATER ETIQUETTE

It is important to remember that all of the people involved in the performance you attend have put lots of work into making the production. The choreographer, dancers, stage technicians and theater managers, just to name a few, work hard to put on a performance. As such, audience members need to respect this work and conduct themselves in a proper manner.

Going to a live dance performance is different from attending a movie, for example. It is appropriate to dress nicely for a performance. Audience members should arrive early to find their seats and should be seated quietly in advance of the rise of the curtain. You should remain in your seat until intermission, and it is not proper to leave early. It is inappropriate to talk during the performance. As students of dance appreciation, you might want to take notes about the performance so that you can remember each piece, but this should be done at intermission.

Cell phones must be turned off and put away during a performance. It is totally inappropriate to talk or to text message until intermission or after the performance. The cell phone should not be used as a light to view the program as this is very distracting to the dancers.

These are simple rules of conduct, but they must be observed so that everyone can enjoy the performance.

Dance as an Art Form

INTRODUCTION

Dance is an art form that is displayed through the human body using the medium of movement. Although there are many definitions, most people involved in dance would agree that dance is a "projection of inner thought and feeling into movement . . ."[1] Dance has the power to communicate and evoke responses. It provides a means for self-expression and enables the participants and viewers to feel and experience the joy of moving.

Throughout history and all around the world, dance has been significant in the lives of many people: from the tribal leader enacting a sacred ritual to the professional dancer who has dedicated his or her life to dance to the person who takes a dance class just for fun. Take, for example, the role that dance plays in the life of the average college student. In talking with college students and asking the question "What is your idea of a fun night out?," many enthusiastically reply "Going out dancing with friends!" It is interesting to note that although this activity seems to be exciting to many college-age students (as well as other age groups), most of them have never actually seen a "professional" dance concert and are also not aware of the rich and lengthy history of dance.

DANCE AND SOCIETY

Imagine a city block anywhere in the nation. Cars and buses fill the streets, the sidewalks are jammed with people and the rattle of the subway trains can be felt underfoot as the crowds pass on top of the grates. A variety of noises fill the air—horns honking, police car sirens, people yelling, a loud radio.

Here, in this city, dance can be found in many different places. At one corner, on the fifth floor of a tall building, is a dance studio. Couples learn how to ballroom dance. Among the participants are members of different age groups, including older couples reliving the dances of their youth, gliding effortlessly across the floor. There are also younger couples experiencing ballroom dance for the first time, struggling with the elegance and precision demanded of this dance form. Across the street, in another studio, is a group of professional dancers taking a ballet class. Nervous energy abounds in the room as an artistic director of a major ballet company looks on, picking out the lucky few who will audition for the

Dance is an art form that is displayed through the human body using the medium of movement.

1

company. Down the street, a billboard advertises the opening of one of the world's most popular modern dance companies. The bold picture of a dancer caught in midair is striking and catches the attention of everyone who passes by. And on the other corner, a group of teenagers practice the latest hip-hop moves, their exuberant athleticism and lightning-fast footwork awing an audience of out-of-towners.

Forty miles outside the city is a rural community, where rolling hills, tall trees and green grass can be seen for miles. There is a peaceful calm and an almost lazy quality about the place. But all over this community there is plenty of dance activity. Today, the local senior center provides instruction in square dancing and each group cheers as the caller successfully navigates them through an intricate series of do-si-dos and promenades. At the elementary school, a guest teacher conducts a creative movement workshop with the students. At first the boys and girls are shy and apprehensive about dancing in front of each other, but they abandon all shyness when the teacher asks them to move like their favorite cartoon character. In the evening, the local high school will perform their annual musical theatre performance, filled with several show-stopping song and dance numbers. And in the neighboring town, the local performing arts council sponsors a dance concert, which will be performed by an African dance company. The concert will be filled with beautifully decorated, authentic African costumes, dynamic and powerfully charged movements and rhythmic drumming.

Dance is recognized as being one of the oldest art forms known to the world.

In between the city and the countryside is a suburb. Neat houses line the streets and the voices and laughter of children can be heard. The neighborhood park is crowded with children who jump, run, skip, leap, roll, hop, and crawl. Although they are not actually dancing, one can clearly see the dance-like quality of their movements and how easily these movements present the opportunity for uninhibited self-expression. During the morning church service, liturgical dancers will perform as part of the mass. They will dance in the processional and will also interpret the day's reading through movement. In the afternoon, a family will gather to celebrate a Bar Mitzvah. They will perform traditional Hebrew dances that have been done for centuries at such occasions. The local dance studio down the street is giving lessons in the latest country and western line dances and hoots and hollers can be heard above the country music. And a world-renowned jazz and tap ensemble will perform tonight at the newly renovated performing arts center, where the syncopated rhythms of the taps will be a perfect complement to the rhythmic jazz music.

Dance can be found in many places, from the most populated to the most rural areas. From the earliest, most primitive cultures to today, every age has had its dance. Dance is recognized as being one of the oldest art forms known to the world and as dance writer and teacher Margaret H'Doubler pointed out, the fact that dance has lived on for thousands of years shows evidence of its value.[2] In order to fully understand the value of dance in society and to understand why it has lived on for so many years, it would be beneficial to look back at what we know to be the beginnings of dance—that of the primitive cultures—and to examine the cultures that followed.

THE PRIMITIVE PERIOD: TO 3000 B.C.

One of the strongest pieces of evidence proving that dance existed in primitive cultures was discovered in a series of rock paintings depicting dance. Primitive peoples created these paintings tens of thousands of years ago (most likely during the Paleolithic Age) in France.[3] Although the information regarding this artifact is not extensive, it still points to the fact that movement played a role in early societies. Since the discovery of these rock paintings, several other drawings and carvings have been found that depict dance in primitive societies. For example, archaeologists discovered a wall painting in a tomb from the fifth dynasty of Giza (created circa 2700 B.C.), which depicted a harvest dance.[4] Also, "Paleolithic cave drawings near Palermo in Sicily depict human figures performing what appears to be ritualistic dance, an observation that implies dance must have been taught and learned."[5] Through much research by leading historians and by studying current uses of dance in several primitive cultures, we know that in these cultures people used dance as a means of communication and as a way of life.

In the absence of a common verbal language, people used their bodies to express thoughts and feelings. Movements and gestures became an essential part of all facets of primitive people's lives. Life's daily rhythms, to which primitive people had a strong connection (internal rhythms, such as breathing, walking and the beat of one's heart, and external rhythms, such as the cycle of day and night and the change of the seasons), were a natural precursor to dancing and singing.

One of the most important aspects of their lives—where dance was used as the ultimate means of expression—was during dance rituals. People used rituals to worship and appease the gods and believed that these rituals held magical and spiritual powers. The occasion of a birth, marriage or death required that a dance ritual be performed in conjunction with the event. These rituals held great meaning for the participants and the viewers. For example, in some primitive societies, a dance ritual held at birth would ensure a long, healthy life for the infant. A marriage ritual would celebrate the transition from single to married life (much like our own traditional wedding ceremony). A ritual at someone's death would ensure that the deceased's spirit would rest peacefully. Probably the most important rituals that occurred in primitive society were those that revolved around fertility (for food and children). Many fertility rituals were done to ask the gods for rain, sunshine, an abundant harvest and healthy children.

It is sometimes hard for contemporary society to understand the magnitude of dance rituals and to see how much early humans' lives revolved around them. It is also difficult to visualize what these dances looked like. Many writers, such as Margaret H'Doubler, state that the movements were very basic; such as running, hopping, swaying, stomping and clapping. The movements were also imitative, devoted to the mimicry of animals, forces of nature and of the gods.[6] The length of the rituals varied, depending on their function. Some lasted only hours, whereas others were conducted over a period of several days.

Today, there are cultures (still considered to be "primitive") that continue to incorporate dance in their daily lives. One example of such people are the *Yanomamo* in the northern part of South America. The *Yanomamo,* mostly found in parts of Venezuela, Brazil, Guyana and Colombia, incorporate many dancing rituals into their lives. According to anthropologist Napoleon Chagnon, one such ritual is called *amoamo* and is performed before a hunt.[7] The men in the tribe do this ritual of song and dance to ensure good luck in capturing and killing animals for food and in anticipation of a feast. The movements typical of the *Yanomamo* rituals are usually high powered and dynamically charged. Chagnon describes one ritual that he witnessed:

> *Two at a time, the . . . dancers entered, pranced around the village periphery, wildly showing off their decorations and weapons and then returning to the group. Each dancer had unique decorations and a unique dance step, something personal that he could exhibit. He would burst into the village screaming a memorized phrase, wheel and spin, stop in his tracks, dance in place, throw his weapons down, pick them up again, aim them at the line of [people] with a wild expression on his face, prance ahead a few steps, repeat his performance and continue on around the village in this manner, while the [people] cheered wildly.[8]*

It is fascinating to examine indigenous societies today and to analyze how they have continued performing the dance rituals that their ancestors did thousands of years ago (obviously not in the exact same way, but probably with the same ritualistic significance). Why did the cultures continue performing these dances? Why did they keep the dance rituals? Why do they still hold so much importance today? The answers to these questions might seem simplistic to people in contemporary society. But for cultures so steeped in tradition, ritual and spirituality, negating these dances would not even be a consideration.

We have seen how dance and movement were prevalent in primitive cultures, and today it remains important to those indigenous cultures still in existence. But, obviously, other cultures developed throughout the ages. For this discussion, we will focus on the broad categories of Ancient, Medieval, Renaissance and Contemporary, although the reader should realize that there are periods within these ages (such as the Baroque period during the Renaissance) in which different styles and dance aesthetics were developed. The reader should also realize that the titles of these periods are Western terms, and that other countries label these time periods differently. For example, what is known as the Medieval era in the West would coincide with the periods that fall between the Northern and Southern Dynasties and the Ming Dynasty in China, and the Yamato and Ashikaga periods in Japan.

In this brief overview, it is important to examine how dance continued throughout the ages and to see how dance developed. For example, when did it take on shape and form, and begin to hold artistic significance? As cultures became "civilized" (such as those of Mesopotamia, Egypt and Asia, who began to make significant developments in writing, government and agriculture), people began to become more aware of how dance was presented. In other words, people began to pay attention to technique (form, content and style), and also to the appearance of dance. Although rituals remained important, many were replaced by ceremonies.[9] Ceremonies were more highly structured and stylized than the spontaneous expression of the ritual, and the dance, whether serving a spiritual function or done for entertainment, was now seen more as an artistic product.

When referring to the different ages, it is important to remember that there are not specific moments in time when one age stopped existing and another one began. There were long periods of overlap between them, and the aesthetic sensibilities of each age permeated the next. These were also complex societies, with long, rich histories. What follows are brief descriptions of each age, highlighting the primary aesthetic and value placed on dance in the societies.

THE ANCIENT PERIOD: ABOUT 3000 B.C. TO 400 A.D.

The dances of the Ancient civilizations were described as "thought . . . combined with dramatic intent, and aesthetic elements were consciously sought."[10] In other words, conscious decisions began to be made with regard to dance. How the dance *looked* and what the dance was to *represent* dictated what movement choices were made. In this age, development of vocal language, as well as the invention of writing, agricultural advancements, centralized government, organized religion and class distinctions all helped to shape these aesthetics. It would be difficult in this brief description to discuss the dance aesthetics of all the societies of Ancient times (including those in the Middle East, Asia, Africa, the Mediterranean, Greece and Rome). Therefore, a few descriptions of dance in ancient times will be included.

India has one of the longest and richest traditions of dance. Archaeologists have found a wealth of evidence that proves that dance was a part of the lives of India's earliest civilizations (2300–1750 B.C.), most likely in the form of religious celebrations.[11] The dance and theatre that was developed in India in ancient times had a great impact on the dance developed throughout all of Asia. One of the places that dance appeared was in the Sanskrit dramas that flourished between the first and tenth centuries. These dramas were religious in nature and reinforced the beliefs and practices of the ancient culture. Around 500–300 B.C., a new dance technique was developed called *Bharata Natyam*. *Bharata Natyam* was a temple dance that required skill, grace and stamina. It is still practiced today (see Figure 1.1) and is known for its flowing arm movements, exact head and eye gestures and complex rhythms that are stamped out by quickly moving feet. There are also records of many types of religious dances, court dances and folk dances, some that lasted well past ancient times and some (like *Bharata Natyam*) that are still practiced today.

China also has records of early dance. A wall painting from the Central Henan Province, dating back to about 200 A.D., depicts a large-scale banquet with dance, juggling and musical performances taking place between the two rows of guests.[12] Today, much of what is known about China's dance comes from the Beijing Opera (formally Peking Opera, which can be traced back to the eighth century), but it is also known that dance was part of many theatrical performances of ancient times. Dance dramas were also performed, with many of the lead characters portrayed as the gods and heroes found in Chinese myths.

In much of Ancient Greece, the ideas of beauty and knowledge dominated the age, and dance, poetry and education were part of daily life. The artistic high point of the Greek period (and perhaps of Ancient times in general) was the fifth century B.C., when the Greek sense of art and beauty provided artistic and spiritual satisfaction for society. This period (along with the later Roman period) is sometimes referred to in other art forms as the "Classical" period.

The development of most Greek dances can be traced back to religious rituals. These dances combined movement, music and poetry, and were often participatory

Figure 1.1
One of India's most famous dancers, Indrani, demonstrates a movement from the *Bharata Natyam* style of dance. Jerome Robbins Dance Division, The New York Public Library for the Performing Arts, Astor, Lenox and Tilden Foundations.

group dances, where people were linked together by holding arms or hands. There were also animal dances, which were probably carried over from primitive times when the mimicry of animals was part of sacred rituals. Dance was also found in the popular Greek theatre, where it was used to emphasize the tragic or comedic aspect of the performance. Today, references to dancing in Ancient Greece can be found in Greek myths, literature, musical notations and on many art objects, such as carvings, sculptures and statues (see Figure 1.2).

THE MEDIEVAL PERIOD: ABOUT 400 A.D. TO 1400 A.D.

During the Medieval era (also referred to as the Middle Ages), we again see many different examples of dance. Some of the most interesting dances during this time are those of the Islamic cultures. The Islamic lands flourished during the Medieval era, and dance was part of both rituals and daily life. There was a traditional form of dance that may have been developed during the ninth and tenth centuries, when Baghdad was the cultural center of Islam.[13] This type of dancing is still

Figure 1.2
Neo Attic Relief *Dancing Maidens* (Spartan Dance), Greco Roman, First Century B.C. The Jerome Robbins Dance Division, the New York Public Library for the Performing Arts, Astor, Lenox and Tilden Foundations.

performed today, and is characterized by an undulating torso, swaying and rocking hips and other rhythmic full-body and arm movements. In Islamic countries, this dance has many different names, and Westerners usually refer to it as "belly dancing," although it would never be called that by the people of the Middle East. Many folk dances were also part of Medieval Islamic culture, some of which are still performed today.

After the fall of the Roman Empire, the idea and importance of art, beauty and aesthetics that was seen in Greece and throughout much of Europe eventually changed under the rule of the Christian church (again, because of the complexity of this era, a broad leap has been taken regarding much of the historical aspects of this period). Although many of the common people took part in folk dance activities, such as the Maypole dance, these dances were seen by the church as pagan activities. The creation of almost *any* art was frowned upon and even banned, unless it was created specifically for the purpose of glorifying the church (for example, the *Mystery Plays,* which are still performed every four years in York, England). While in the past, the development of the intellect was the main focus, now the enhancement of spirituality was the priority. "Dance, both because it was pleasurable and because it was physical, was frowned upon and all but suppressed in secular life, and was permitted to exist only in the staid form as a part of . . . worship."[14] Any non-religious dances (such as folk dances, which were at that time performed as rituals and for entertainment) were generally performed covertly.

The church dictated much of what happened in society. The church placed a great emphasis on the idea that the body was evil, and that the purity of the soul was the only thing that mattered. This idea, along with the outbreak of the Black (bubonic) Plague (around 1347), led to a preoccupation with death and dying, superstitions and witchcraft. Margaret H'Doubler noted that this side of medieval-ism tended to be fanatical and unbalanced, and in extreme cases led to a dancing frenzy:

> *The dancing mania that swept over Europe during and immediately after the Black Death [a disease that killed as much as half the population of Europe] was no new disease, but a phenomenon well known to the Middle Ages . . . Men, women, and young boys and girls would dance in wild delirium, seemingly possessed and without any will of their own.*[15]

Many historians have written about this dancing mania, commonly referred to as the Dance of Death or *Danse Macabre*. There are different theories as to why this dancing mania occurred. Some speculate that these outbursts were truly part of a physical disorder caused by the plague, while others feel these dancing manias were in direct response to an extreme feeling of dread and to the overwhelming control that the church placed upon the society. Others believe they were due to a mental disorder that afflicted people across Europe, while still others believe that it was due to a combination of the above. Whatever the reason, the idea of death obsessed many people, and much of the art created during this time centered around the death figure, usually portrayed as a skeleton or a group of skeletons.

In spite of the church and the Black Plague, dance did continue, and by the end of the Middle Ages was beginning to be seen in theatrical performances and at balls. The revival of dance as an art form was an important part of the general rebirth of the arts that is associated with the Renaissance period.

The revival of dance as an art form was an important part of the general rebirth of the arts that is associated with the Renaissance period.

THE RENAISSANCE PERIOD: ABOUT 1400 A.D. TO 1700 A.D.

Dance held much importance in the Renaissance period. In the West, this period was ". . . an expression of renewed interest in the culture of the ancient world . . . art became less and less a group activity and more and more the creative product of individual artists."[16] Court ballets were developed in this age, beginning in the fifteenth and sixteenth centuries, and folk dancing continued to be a popular means of expression for the working classes. Instrumental music became the accompaniment for many social dances, such as the minuet, pavan, allemande, and saraband, to name a few (see Figure 1.3). These dances, also known as pre-classic dances, were performed in the courts, and were a combination of "common" folk dances and the aristocratic steps of the nobility.

Figure 1.3
The Minuet from
Kellom Tomlinson's
The Art of Dancing
(1724). The Jerome
Robbins Dance Divi-
sion, the New York
Public Library for the
Performing Arts,
Astor, Lenox and
Tilden Foundations.

The Renaissance period saw the rise of ballet as a professional art form, one
that continued to develop throughout the seventeenth and eighteenth centuries. The
birth of the Romantic ballet occurred during the nineteenth century. This ballet
style followed the aesthetic that was already occurring in music, literature, painting and sculpture (see *Chapter 2: Ballet*). Also during this time, some of the
world's most captivating dance traditions were developed, many of which are still
in existence today.

THE CONTEMPORARY PERIOD: 1700 TO THE PRESENT

While Eastern countries continued to perform traditional dances and create new
dances based on tradition elements, contemporary times have seen the develop-

ment of many dance genres (particularly in the West). The early part of the twentieth century introduced classical and contemporary ballet, as well as modern dance (since the majority of this book covers these major developments, no further discussion of specific dance genres is needed here). The twentieth century presented society with many advancements. Just as technology and science became more sophisticated, so did art; so did dance. As discussed throughout this book, the twentieth century presented the world with some of the greatest dance artists and dances ever known. And as we are finding in the twenty-first century, there is no shortage of artistic and innovative dance artists.

Throughout the Ancient, Medieval, Renaissance and Contemporary ages, dance underwent many changes; from being an intellectual endeavor to being banned as a pagan activity. From being the cultural undertaking of the nobility to being the artistic voice of the working class. From being a spectacle of beautiful poses, costumes and grace, to being a forum for social and political messages.

From primitive times to today, dance has remained relevant in most societies. The importance that dance held in these societies, however, has differed from age to age and culture to culture. Today, while many people view dance as merely something to do or watch for entertainment purposes, others see dance as a viable and important art form. Although entertainment is a part of dance, it is not its most essential reason for being. Therefore, in order to understand the true meaning of dance, we must first understand dance as an art form.

Although entertainment is a part of dance, it is not its most essential reason for being. Therefore, in order to understand the true meaning of dance, we must first understand dance as an art form.

ART AND THE AESTHETIC EXPERIENCE

When an artist creates (in dance, the creator is the choreographer), he or she usually creates in order to present something before an audience. More specifically, the artist wants to *communicate* something to the audience. Regardless of whether the created work is literal or abstract, the desire and need for self-expression propels the artist to create. Therefore, many times when viewing a work of art (whether it is a dance, painting, sculpture, poem, etc.), the audience is being challenged by the creator of the work to *think* about what the work of art represents or evokes. Choreographer and writer Agnes de Mille stated that works of art are "symbols through which people communicate what lies beyond ordinary speech . . . art is communication on the deepest and most lasting level."[17] Often, people will view art and quickly say "I like it," or "I don't like it," without ever knowing why. It is everyone's right and privilege to be critical of a work or to not like it, but "knee-jerk" reactions to art, whether they be positive or negative, are not expressing an informed opinion. If the viewer will take the time, however, to examine an artist's work with objectivity and with an open mind, they might connect with what the artist is trying to communicate or represent. This "connection" can be a very rewarding and satisfying experience, but can also be a thought-provoking or sometimes uncomfortable one. For example, if a person views a dance that the choreographer intended to be about love and the viewer is also in love, then this dance might produce a very pleasurable feeling. But what if the viewer has just ended a long-term relationship? For that person, this dance might be very sad and even hard to watch. If de Mille is accurate in saying that "art is communication on the deepest and lasting level," then one of the purposes of art is to illuminate for the viewer those things in life that touch us at the deepest core of our being. We relate to what we see in a work of art by using our aesthetic sense—perceiving something through feelings. Similarly, the feelings evoked from viewing a work of art can be said to produce an "aesthetic experience."

When viewing a work of art, an individual may have an aesthetic experience. A work can be said to be aesthetically pleasing when it evokes responses from the viewer with little conscious reasoning. These responses are not limited to things that make people feel happy, or to things that people consider to be beautiful, as we discovered in the example of the dance choreographed about love. We now know that a dance that has a dark and dramatic theme, such as death, can have a strong aesthetic appeal to an audience, even though it may make them feel uncomfortable. It is important to remember that the interaction with the work of art must *do something to the viewer*. This "something" may be either a physical reaction (such as a "nervous" feeling in one's stomach), or an emotional reaction (such as happiness or sadness). The work of art must move the viewer in some way, either positively or negatively.[18]

Obviously, what one person considers to be aesthetically pleasing, another may not. How do people view art and what makes them decide what is aesthetically pleasing or moving? Many human characteristics and traits are factors in determining this answer. For example, a person's moral, religious and ethical values may be a key factor in determining what he or she has an aesthetic response to. Also, an individual's intellect, imagination, tastes and personal experiences may play a role, as may the amount of education a person has had. The socioeconomic background of a person may be another factor, as well as his or her emotional state (in general and at the time of viewing the work of art).

To illustrate this point more clearly, it might be beneficial to look at some hypothetical situations. Do you think a person from a conservative background might view a work of art (let's say a painting) that contained nudity differently than a person with a liberal background? Maybe, maybe not. What if a live dance that they were watching contained nudity? What if the dance contained references to alternative lifestyles? As in life, the more controversial or foreign things are to what we know, the more we either question it, accept it or push it aside. It is not possible, nor particularly desirable, for people to put aside the characteristics that comprise their emotional makeup when viewing a work of art. It is important, however, that people view art with an open mind and provide time for themselves to react to the work in an intelligent manner.

In addition to individual people having their own aesthetic sense, society (as a whole or as different groups) can also have a particular aesthetic opinion. As people and times change, so will values and tastes. For example, several of our most treasured works of art were shunned by many in their respective societies. Composer Igor Stravinsky's *Le Sacre Du Printemps (The Rite of Spring)* caused a commotion the first time it was performed before an audience in 1913. With choreography by Vaslav Nijinsky, the ballet, performed in Paris, received boos and hisses from the time the music started until the final curtain (in addition to a near riot almost breaking out in the theatre). People reacted this way because the music and dance were different from *anything* that they had ever heard or seen before. The music had harsh and uneven rhythms and the choreography played upon those rhythms with movements that pounded and stamped the floor, employed turned-in legs and used sharp, angular gestures. The audience saw it as outrageous

Remember that the interaction with the work of art must do something to the viewer.

It is important that people view art with an open mind and provide time for themselves to react to the work in an intelligent manner.

and unacceptable. Today, both the music and the choreography of *Le Sacre Du Printemps* are regarded as outstanding works of art.

Another example are the plays of Henrik Ibsen that were produced in the late 1800s and were, for the most part, hated by the European community because of the content and the style in which they were written. Ibsen dealt frankly with issues (such as moral hypocrisy and the oppression of women) that a complacent society preferred to keep hidden. Today, the plays of Ibsen are produced throughout the world, and he is considered one of the outstanding playwrights in the history of dramatic literature. It is important to remember that works of art do not become better or worse over time, they simply look different and have a different value, as society changes.

Works of art do not become better or worse over time, they simply look different and have a different value, as society changes.

SUMMARY

From the earliest ritual dances of primitive cultures to the most sophisticated work of contemporary artists, dance has had a long, rich history. Philosopher Susanne Langer described dance in this way:

> . . . *dance, like any other work of art, is a perceptible form that expresses the nature of human feeling—the rhythms and connections, crises and breaks, the complexity and richness of what is sometimes called [humanity's] "inner life," the stream of direct experience, life as it feels to the living.*[19]

Though today many tend to view dance simply as a form of entertainment, it has the potential to significantly raise an audience's awareness, inviting them to think and feel in new and different ways. Of course, each individual's reaction to a dance will be determined, to an extent, by what that individual brings to the dance—an audience's response to a dance says as much about the audience as it does the dance. Table 1.1 outlines the details of dance within various time periods.

TABLE 1.1 DANCE THROUGH THE AGES

DANCE IN THE PRIMITIVE PERIOD	DANCE IN THE ANCIENT PERIOD	DANCE IN THE MEDIEVAL PERIOD	DANCE IN THE RENAISSANCE PERIOD
—Dance was used as a means of communication. —Dance rituals were done to worship and appease the gods. —Dance rituals were done at special occasions, such as a birth, marriage or death. —Many dance rituals focused on fertility and having an abundant harvest. —Movements were imitative (of nature and animals) and very basic.	—Aesthetic elements were consciously sought. —Developments and advancements in writing, agriculture and government helped to shape the dance aesthetic. —Movement choices were made in order to represent certain themes. —The height of the Ancient period was the Greek period, fifth century B.C., when the quest for art and beauty was the priority. —Many Greek dances developed out of religious rituals. —Dances combined movement, music and poetry and were often participatory. —Dance was often found in the popular Greek Theatre. —Many dances of India were religious dances. *Bharata Natyam* developed as a temple dance. —Evidence of dance in China dates back to 200 A.D. The dances performed in eighth-century China influenced all of the dance that was to follow.	—In most of Europe, the church saw dance as a pagan activity. —Dance was banned unless it glorified the church. —The Black Plague killed as much as half the population of Europe and led to a preoccupation with death and dying, superstitions and witchcraft. The Dance of Death emerged at this time. —In Islamic lands dance flourished during this time and was done for rituals and for entertainment purposes.	—A renewed interest in the arts developed. —Dance became less of a group activity and more about the individual artist. —Court ballets flourished and folk dancing remained popular with the working class. —Ballet emerged as a professional art form (see *Chapter 5: Ballet*).

2

Ballet

INTRODUCTION

Ballet is an art form that has a long, rich history dating back to the fifteenth century. One of the earliest records of balletic movements comes from a book of dance instruction created by a dancing master named Domenico da Piacenza.[1] Perhaps a more significant moment in ballet history—one that would pave the way for the art form from the sixteenth century to the present—was the arrival of Catherine de' Medici (1519–1589) in France. She came to France from her native Italy to marry into the ruling family of Henri, Duc d'Orleans, who would later become the King of France. When de' Medici came to France, she brought with her several Italian dancing masters. Along with these dancing masters, she introduced a new type of entertainment to the public, later to be known as the court ballet. Balthasar de Beaujoyeulx (c. 1535–1587) was de' Medici's head dancing master. In 1573, he created the *Ballet des Polonais,* a court entertainment performed by sixteen women who each represented one of the French provinces. Beaujoyeulx went on to create the *Ballet Comique de la Reine*, which many historians point to as the first court ballet. It was produced in 1581 and was described in the following way:

> [The] ballet by [dancing master] Beaujoyeulx . . . was commissioned by Catherine de' Medici . . .
> The spectacle lasted from 10:00 P.M. to 3:30 A.M. The ballet was chiefly concerned with the legend
> of Circe and part of the set represented the Garden and Castle of Circe. The principal dancers were
> a group of twelve Naiads, danced by a princess and several duchesses . . . Musicians sat in a golden
> vault, framed by clouds lighted from the inside . . . The cost of the spectacle was 3,600,000 gold
> francs. The libretto of the ballet was published in 1582 and was to become one of the first books on
> ballet.[2]

EARLY BALLET

The "ballets" presented in the sixteenth century were very different from today's ballets. As the above description shows, the court ballets were very much a feast for the eyes. These dazzling spectacles were a marvel to see, even though they sometimes consisted only of simple floor patterns and poses. Elaborate costumes were the rule, although they greatly restricted the performer's movements. These ballets progressed at a leisurely pace, sometimes lasting several hours.

Ballet is an art form that has a long, rich history dating back to the fifteenth century.

The court ballets were performed by and for members of the nobility. The most prominent of these nobles was Louis XIV (1638–1715), commonly referred to as the Sun King. He was the King of France from 1643–1715 and during that time commissioned many ballets in which he himself performed. In 1661, he granted permission to several dancing masters to establish The Royal Academy of Dance in France and the development of the court ballet flourished. This academy later became known as the Paris Opera, which still exists today.

At the end of the sixteenth century, with the creation of the proscenium stage (that separated the audience from the performer), ballet began to take on a more serious and theatrical quality. Dancers began to use a "turned-out" position (rotating the legs out at the hip joint) in order to move more efficiently. A set vocabulary of movements was developed, which included positions of the feet, arms and head, as well as locomotor (moving) and non-locomotor (in-place) movements. Thus, a rigorous technique was developed, one that required a dancer to train daily for many hours in order to become truly proficient. The new priorities set in the sixteenth century gained momentum and by the seventeenth century, ballet was recognized as a viable art form. Dance masters vigorously trained dancers to perform with technical proficiency and many ballets were created based on this principle.

In the eighteenth century, however, the ballet aesthetic began to change. The emphasis that had been placed on technique was no longer the priority. People began to feel that the *meaning* or *message* that the movements depicted were the most important element of dance. Therefore, the priority was placed on having the audience "feel" something and receive a message from the performance.

During this time, Jean Georges Noverre (1727–1810) developed *ballet d' action*. This concept brought the importance of having a plot and using emotion in dance to the forefront of ballet choreography. He also wrote *Letters on Dancing and Ballet*, which defended ballet as a high art form—one that he felt had the power to communicate even more effectively than words.

The nineteenth century produced the Romantic ballet. "Romanticism was characterized by a passionate striving to discover meaning in human events, an effort that was uniquely reflected in all of the romantic arts, but most perfectly in its ballet."[3] Dance began to follow the path that had been set up by the Romantic artists of music, literature, painting and sculpture. Their style of art was characterized by a number of different elements, such as love of nature, emotion, power, violence and tranquility. The Romantic ballets, although they contained those same elements, were characterized by their use of mythical characters and places, which created atmospheres of great wonder and excitement. These ballets also featured the female dancer.

One of the first Romantic ballets to be performed was *La Sylphide* (1832), choreographed by Filippo Taglioni (1777–1871). Although this ballet is occasionally performed today, the ballet *Giselle* is the one that is synonymous with the Romantic era. Today many ballet companies all around the world perform *Giselle*. Choreographed in 1841 by Jean Coralli and Jules Perrot, *Giselle* depicts the story of a woman who dies of a broken heart and comes back as a "wilis" (a mythical spirit figure), not to seek revenge on her lover, but to protect him from the evil wilis.

From the fifteenth to the nineteenth century, there were great shifts in the desired aesthetics of the ballet world, and these shifts were a trend that would continue into the twentieth century. In the late 1800s, ballet took on a new look, philosophy and aesthetic, which is referred to as "classical" ballet. Similarly, the early 1900s marked the advent of "contemporary" ballet. These two styles have remained popular and have shaped the history and ballet aesthetic of modern times.

Although there are different styles of ballet within the classical and contemporary genres, certain similarities of form do exist (see the *Summary*). There is, for example, a universal movement vocabulary that is shared by all forms of ballet. The steps (all employing the French language) remain the same from country to country. A person who only speaks one language could go to *any* country and teach ballet and would probably be perfectly understood, assuming that everyone present was familiar with the ballet terminology. As we have seen, certain differences, stylistic and historic, have separated ballet into two categories—classical and contemporary.

CLASSICAL BALLET

The history of classical ballet can be traced back to the late 1800s in Russia when choreographer Marius Petipa (1818–1910) began to create ballets. Several characteristics and features are always found in a classical ballet. The most obvious is the overall "look" of the ballet. Performed on a proscenium stage, spectacular scenery usually fills the upstage (farthest point away from the audience) and side areas of the stage. The dancers are always dressed in elaborate costumes typical of the characters they are portraying. These factors enhance the storyline of the ballet, which is usually a fairy-tale or fable. For example, *The Sleeping Beauty*, choreographed in 1890 by Marius Petipa and first performed in Russia, tells the story of the young princess Aurora who is put under a spell by the evil fairy Carabosse. As we know from the Mother Goose version, under the spell the princess falls asleep, never to awake again. The kiss of a prince revives her, however, and they live happily ever after. Another classical ballet entitled *Swan Lake,* choreographed by Marius Petipa and Lev Ivanov in 1895 (the first *Swan Lake,* choreographed by Wenzel Reisinger in 1877 for the Bolshoi Theatre, was not successful), also first performed in Russia, tells the story of a swan, Odette, who is changed to a beautiful woman for a brief period of time by a mysterious sorcerer named Von Rotbart. She meets and falls in love with Prince Siegfried. The two can never be together, however, because Odette is under the powerful spell of Von Rotbart. In the end, both Odette and Siegfried realize that they can only be together in the afterlife and they both throw themselves into a lake. This ballet has an uncharacteristically sad ending for a classical ballet, but is one of the most popular ever created.

Another characteristic of classical ballet is the use of music. The choreographer brings the music to life by creating the steps to "move along" with the music. For example, if the music was in 3/4 or "waltz" time, the choreographer would follow this rhythm with the movement, paying close attention to the counts, phrasing, accents and crescendos. Large orchestral pieces of music are the norm for a classical ballet. Although there are many composers who have created music specifically for ballets, there are two particularly prominent Russian-born composers who are known throughout the ballet world. Igor Stravinsky and Peter Tchaikovsky have both created some of today's best-loved orchestrations. Some

Several characteristics and features are always found in a classical ballet. The most obvious is the overall "look" of the ballet.

Large orchestral pieces of music are the norm for a classical ballet.

of the contemporary ballets that Stravinsky created musical compositions for are *The Firebird* (1910), choreographed by Michel Fokine; *Rite of Spring* (1913), choreographed by Vaslav Nijinsky; and *Les Noces* (1923), choreographed by Bronislava Nijinska. Tchaikovsky's compositions for classical ballets include *Swan Lake* (1877), choreographed by Marius Petipa and Lev Ivanov; *The Sleeping Beauty* (1890), choreographed by Marius Petipa; and *The Nutcracker* (1892), choreographed by Lev Ivanov. Other popular composers such as Claude Debussy, Maurice Ravel, Erik Satie and Serge Prokofiev have also created musical scores that were (and are) used in ballet choreography.

The use of dancers in classical repertory is similar from ballet to ballet. For classical repertory, the dancers are usually divided into three categories—the principals (who have the leading roles in the ballets), the soloists (who have solo and character roles) and the *corps de ballet* (the remaining members of the company). The principals, particularly the male and female leads, are always the main focus of the ballet and are the dancers who move the storyline from beginning to end (see Figure 2.1). The climax and most proscribed moment of classical ballet is the

Figure 2.1
Margot Fonteyn and Michael Somes in *Swan Lake, Act II*; 1953. Jerome Robbins Dance Division, The New York Public Library for the Performing Arts, Astor, Lenox and Tilden Foundations.

grand pas de deux, or step for two. The *grand pas de deux* follows a specific format, beginning with the entrance of the male and female dancers, who then perform an *adagio* (slow duet). This *adagio* is followed by a variation (solo) for each dancer, beginning with the male, that is usually comprised of difficult and quick movements. The two dancers then return together for a final coda (or final movements) to complete the *grand pas de deux.* The female dancer, or ballerina, is the main focus of the duet parts of the *pas de deux.* The role of the male dancer is to support her in the difficult turns and lifts that are found in most classical ballet repertoires.

The corps serves almost as part of the elaborate scenery, sometimes standing perfectly still in a pose for minutes at a time while the principals and/or soloists dance downstage (closest to the audience). Usually the corps are costumed to look exactly alike and execute the same movements at the same time. Their movements on stage are usually very linear and their floor patterns give a balanced and symmetrical look to the stage space.

Pantomime and the use of literal gestures is often seen in classical ballets. For example, if a male dancer wanted to pantomime "I love you," he might point to himself, put his hands over his heart and then point at the person that he loves. As classical ballets always feature a strong storyline, pantomime is often utilized to ensure that the plot remains intelligible to the audience.

In classical ballet, the female dancers wear pointe shoes. Pointe shoes are specially designed so that the ballerina can stand directly on the tips of her toes. In professional companies, each ballerina has her shoes made specifically for her. Usually, a pair of pointe shoes lasts for one performance.

CONTEMPORARY BALLET

Contemporary ballet evolved in Russia in the early 1900s due mainly to the work of a choreographer named Michel Fokine (1880–1942). Fokine was the first master choreographer of the Ballet Russes, a Russian company developed in 1909 by Serge Diaghilev (1872–1929). Diaghilev was neither a dancer nor a choreographer, but a producer who had a passion for dance and brought together many of the ballet world's most recognized figures, such as Vaslav Nijinsky, Anna Pavlova (see Figure 2.2), Leonide Massine, Enrico Cecchetti, George Balanchine and others (see "Major Figures in Ballet").

Fokine and Diaghilev shared the same aesthetic, one that pushed the boundaries and introduced a new dance to the public. Fokine had several principles that he infused in all of his choreography. One was that classical steps should be reshaped and modified to fit the theme of a dance. Also, the movement in a dance should give insight into what is happening on stage, therefore pantomime, as seen in classical ballets, should not be used. He felt strongly that the members of the *corps de ballet* be more than just a part of the scenery, but should be an important part of the entire dance. And finally, in keeping with the concept of collaboration developed by Diaghilev, all aspects of the ballet—movement, music, costumes and set—should be presented with equal importance.[4] Fokine's choreography also served to heighten the status of the male dancer in a society that was used to seeing the female as the center of the ballet.

Figure 2.2
Anna Pavlova as the *Dragon Fly.* Jerome Robbins Dance Division, The New York Public Library for the Performing Arts, Astor, Lenox and Tilden Foundations.

Contemporary ballet is similar to classical ballet in that they both use the same vocabulary of movement.

The Ballet Russes not only had Fokine to present a new type of ballet to the masses, but also employed Nijinsky (1889–1950) as a choreographer. Like Fokine, Nijinsky presented a truly contemporary form of ballet, but also used so-called taboo themes in his choreography. In his ballet, *L'Apres-midi d'un Faune* (*The Afternoon of a Faun,* 1912), audiences were shocked to see the overt sexual references, as well as the truly unorthodox choreography, which included two dimensional movements, the use of the parallel leg position and revealing costumes.

Contemporary ballet is similar to classical ballet in that they both use the same vocabulary of movement. Also, the dancers who perform the movements must be highly trained (technically) and must have an outstanding performance quality. The *use* of music is also the same, with much emphasis placed on meter, counts, phrasing, etc., although the musical "styles" used might be very different. For example, contemporary ballet might use music that is abstract (atonal, having mixed-meters), whereas classical would not. The female dancers, or ballerinas, usually wear pointe shoes while performing, although some contemporary ballets might employ the use of ballet slippers or even bare feet. Choreographers of contemporary ballet reject the use of pantomime and literal gestures and abstract the movements that appear within the dances. Contemporary ballet choreographers also use more freedom of movement in the torso, upper body and arms, giving the movements a more "modern dance" flavor.

Although there are some similarities between classical and contemporary ballet, the differences are striking, with the most prominent being the lack of storyline or plot. Contemporary ballet is usually concerned with movement as the primary focus. Although most of Fokine's and Nijinsky's work usually had a strong narrative, many contemporary choreographers do not hold to this dance aesthetic. One major figure who is known for outstanding contemporary ballet choreography was George Balanchine (1904–1983, see Figure 2.3), a Russian choreographer who

Although there are some similarities between classical and contemporary ballet, the differences are striking, with the most prominent being the lack of storyline or plot.

Figure 2.3
George Balanchine. Jerome Robbins Dance Division, The New York Public Library for the Performing Arts, Astor, Lenox and Tilden Foundations.

worked with the Ballet Russes and in 1933 defected to the United States. Balanchine was one of ballet's greatest innovators and is considered by many to be the greatest contemporary ballet choreographer of our time (his choreography is also referred to as being "neoclassical"). He eliminated the elaborate sets and costumes used in classical ballets (that he felt took the focus away from the dancer's movements) and presented the dancers as equals on stage (not as principals and corps). The typical *grand pas de deux* that was usually seen in classical ballet works was not always seen in his choreography. Instead, he sometimes presented what could more accurately be called "duets" (although they would always be referred to as *pas de deux* in the ballet genre). Balanchine is known for his "plotless" ballets that have as their focus the marriage of movement and music rather than a storyline. Two of his most famous plotless ballets are *Concerto Barocco* (1941) and *Agon* (1957). Balanchine did, however, choreograph some narrative ballets, with two of the most popular being *The Prodigal Son* (1929 and revised in 1950) and *A Midsummer Night's Dream* (1962).

The Balanchine legacy lives on in many of today's leading ballet companies, who perform one or more of his hundreds of dances and full-length ballets. New York City Ballet, which Balanchine began in 1948 with Lincoln Kirstein, is one company whose repertory is made up mostly of dances by Balanchine. Other companies, such as American Ballet Theatre and Dance Theatre of Harlem, perform Balanchine's works on a regular basis.

Today, there are many contemporary ballet choreographers. Maurice Béjart (b.1927) is one of the most recognized contemporary ballet choreographers in the world. Currently the artistic director of The Béjart Ballet, he is recognized for his witty and often flamboyant dances. Operating on the premise that dance is a powerful form of communication, he draws his inspiration to choreograph from different cultures and what he feels are the religious and social aspects of dance. He often blurs male and female identities, which is a trademark of his work. His angular yet elegant movements are also prominent features of his exciting and theatrical dances.

In 1995, London choreographer Matthew Bourne (b.1960) created a version of *Swan Lake* in which all of the swans are male, powerful and aggressive, though the production is also infused with comic moments. Among the many awards he has received for this production are two Tony awards for Direction and Choreography. Bourne's *Swan Lake* has been seen worldwide, and its edgy and inventive choreography has added another dimension to the dance world. Recent projects of Bourne's include choreographing and co-directing Disney's *Mary Poppins* (2004) and a stage version of *Edward Scissorhands* (2005).

There are also many modern dance choreographers who have created works specifically for ballet companies. In 1947, Valerie Bettis (1919–1982) was the first modern dance choreographer to set a work on a ballet company (the Ballet Russes de Monte Carlo). In 1973, Twyla Tharp (b.1942) was invited to choreograph two dances for the Joffrey Ballet; *Deuce Coupe* (which was performed to music by the Beach Boys), and *As Time Goes By*. In 1976, Tharp choreographed *Push Comes to Shove* for the American Ballet Theatre (ABT). The dance starred Mikhail Baryshnikov, who in 1980, became the artistic director of ABT and hired Tharp as a resident choreographer for the company. In 1993, the Joffrey Ballet commissioned four modern and contemporary ballet choreographers to create an evening-length work entitled *Billboards*. *Billboards* featured the music of Prince and was a tremendous box office success.

SUMMARY

Both classical and contemporary ballets are performed all over the world and are as popular today as they were years ago. There are about twenty major nationally and internationally known professional ballet companies in the United States (and *many* smaller regional companies). These companies perform ballets that were created years ago, as well as new ballets. An audience member would quickly be able to recognize if the ballet they were viewing were a classical or contemporary ballet, simply by looking at the costumes, scenery, staging, music and how the dancers are used on stage. The similarities and differences between classical and contemporary ballet can be found in Table 2.1. Refer to Table 2.2 for an outline of ballet events.

TABLE 2.1 THE SIMILARITIES AND DIFFERENCES BETWEEN CLASSICAL AND CONTEMPORARY BALLET

SIMILARITIES	DIFFERENCES
—Both use a vocabulary of movement that employs the French language. —Both emphasize a strong relationship to music. —Both utilize dancers who are highly trained in their technique and performance abilities. —Both the male and female dancers are featured on stage (in the Romantic period, the female dancer took prominence).	—Classical ballet always has a storyline; most contemporary ballets focus on the movement. —Classical ballet appears very symmetrical, with both sides of the stage equally "balanced" by having the same number of dancers on each side executing the same movements. Contemporary ballet does not focus on symmetry, and having a stage that is "unbalanced" is a characteristic of the style. —Classical ballets are always danced to classical music. Contemporary ballets may also use this type of music, but can also use music that is abstract or from a specific genre, such as jazz music. —There is always a *pas de deux* in classical ballet; there may or may not be one in contemporary ballet. —Classical ballet choreography may incorporate pantomime and literal gestures; contemporary ballet never does. —Female dancers always wear pointe shoes in a classical ballet; they may or may not wear them in contemporary ballet. —For the most part, dancers in a classical ballet keep their spines erect; dancers in a contemporary ballet curve, twist and bend their upper bodies.

TABLE 2.2 OUTLINE OF BALLET EVENTS

1400–1700	Renaissance Period
1559	Catherine de' Medici brings ballet masters from Italy to France.
1573	Balthasar de Beaujoyeulx, dé Medici's head dancing master, creates *Ballet de Polonais*.
1581	Balthasar de Beaujoyeulx creates *Comique de la Reine*, considered the first court ballet.
1661	Louis XIV, the Sun King, establishes the Royal Academy of Dance.
1661	Pierre Beauchamp creates the five positions of the feet.
1681	The first female ballet dancer appears on stage. Women are now permitted to perform in professional ballets.
1754	Jean Georges Noverre creates his first ballet and eventually brings *ballet d' action* to the forefront of ballet choreography.
1760	Jean Georges Noverre publishes *Letters on Dancing and Ballet*.
1822	Dancing *en pointe* is introduced.
1832	Filippo Taglioni choreographs *La Sylphide*, considered the first Romantic ballet.
1841	Jean Coralli and Jules Perrot choreograph *Giselle*.
1870	Arthur Saint-Léon choreographs *Coppélia*, one of the last great Romantic ballets.
1877	Wenzel Reisinger choreographs the first production of *Swan Lake* for the Bolshoi Theatre. This production was not successful.
1890	Marius Petipa, the father of classical ballet, choreographs *The Sleeping Beauty*.
1895	Marius Petipa and Lev Ivanov choreograph *Swan Lake*, and it is a great success.
1909	The first season of Diaghilev's Ballet Russes.
1909	Diaghilev hires Vaslav Nijinsky, Anna Pavlova and Michel Fokine, the father of contemporary ballet.
1910	The first ballet company in America is established; The Chicago Opera Ballet.
1924	George Balanchine joins the Ballet Russes.
1929	Diaghilev dies.
1933	Balanchine defects to the United States. He begins to develop a ballet company.
1934	George Balanchine and Lincoln Kirstein start the School of American Ballet in Hartford, Conn. It eventually moves to New York.
1937	The Mikhail Mordkin Ballet is established, later to become the American Ballet Theatre.
1947	Valerie Bettis is the first modern dancer to choreograph on a ballet company (The Ballet Russes de Monte Carlo).

(continued)

TABLE 2.2 OUTLINE OF BALLET EVENTS (CONTINUED)

1948	After having a series of ballet companies, Balanchine and Kirstein officially establish The New York City Ballet.
1950	Nijinsky dies.
1967	Arthur Mitchell founds the Dance Theatre of Harlem.
1974	Mikhail Baryshnikov defects to the United States.
1976	Modern dance choreographer Twyla Tharp sets *Push Comes to Shove* on the American Ballet Theatre, with Baryshnikov as the lead dancer.
1977	*The Turning Point*, a movie about ballet starring Baryshnikov, is made.
1980	Baryshnikov becomes artistic director of the American Ballet Theatre.
1983	Balanchine dies and leaves over 460 dances and full-length ballets. Peter Martins becomes artistic director of New York City Ballet.
1985	Baryshnikov and tap dancer Gregory Hines star in the movie *White Nights*, with choreography by Twyla Tharp.
1990	Baryshnikov leaves the American Ballet Theatre and, with modern dance choreographer Mark Morris, begins the White Oak Dance Project, a modern dance repertory company.
1993	The Joffrey Ballet produces *Billboards*, which uses music by Prince and choreography by modern dance and contemporary ballet choreographers Laura Dean, Charles Moultan, Peter Pucci and Margo Sappington. It is a box office success.
1994	American Ballet Theatre dancers form their own union, the Independent Artists of America.
1995	Choreographer Matthew Bourne creates a version of *Swan Lake*, which differs radically from all other versions. The swans in Bourne's ballet are all male, and appear powerful, aggressive and violent. This ballet had successful runs in theatres all around the world.
1999	Seven ballerinas from American Ballet Theatre perform in the Romantic ballet *Giselle*.
2000	American Ballet Theatre debuts in China with a performance of the classical ballet *La Bayadere*.
2001	Christopher Wheeldon is named Resident Choreographer at New York City Ballet.
2003	New York City Ballet holds a year-long celebration of the centennial of George Balanchine's birth. It begins on November 25 and continues through the 2004 season.
2004	The U.S. Postal Service issues stamps honoring four choreographers for their contributions. The stamps honor George Balanchine, Alvin Ailey, Agnes deMille and Martha Graham.
2004	Dance Theatre of Harlem experiences major financial difficulties. Artistic Director Arthur Mitchell begins a massive fund-raising effort, and new Board members are elected. A new Executive Director, Laueen Naidu is hired to help save the company and the Dance Theater of Harlem School.

Major Figures in Ballet

Ballet, which has its roots in the court dances of Italy and later France (sixteenth and seventeenth centuries), has in its long history many outstanding choreographers and dancers. Here is a partial list of some of the artists that helped shape the world of ballet.

THE BEGINNINGS:
SIXTEENTH THROUGH THE EIGHTEENTH CENTURY

CATHERINE DE' MEDICI (1519–1589)—A member of one of Italy's royal families, de' Medici married into the French monarchy. Neither a dancer nor a choreographer, de' Medici had a love for dance and brought several dancing masters with her from Italy to France. Thus began the long reign of the court ballet.

BALTHASAR DE BEAUJOYEULX (c. 1535–1587)—Beaujoyeulx was one of de' Medici's dancing masters. He is credited with producing the *Ballet Comique de la Reine*, the first court ballet of note.

PIERRE BEAUCHAMP (1631–c. 1705)—Beauchamp was a dancing master and the first ballet master of the Academy of Dance in France. He created the five ballet positions used today and also developed the technique of using the turned-out leg. He also devised a system of dance notation.

JEAN BAPTISTE LULLY (1632–1687)—A dancer and composer, Lully was the director of the Royal Academy of Music and Dance, which opened in 1672. Louis XIV granted permission for this academy, which later came to be known as the Paris Opera. Lully was instrumental in elevating the status of opera and ballet in the courts from entertainment to a professional art form.

LOUIS XIV (1638–1715)—Also known as the Sun King, Louis XIV was the King of France from 1643–1715. He was a great lover of dance and appeared in several court ballets. He granted permission to establish the first Academy of Dance.

LOUIS PECOUR (1653–1729)—One of Beauchamp's former students, Pecour succeeded Beauchamp as director of the *Paris Opera*. He also introduced the minuet to the nobility of France.

JOHN WEAVER (1673–1760)—Weaver was an English choreographer who published the first written history of ballet. He also was the first choreographer to employ the use of pantomime in his ballets.

FRANCOISE PREVOST (1680–1741)—A star of the Paris Opera, Prevost was also an outstanding teacher. She was mostly known for her dramatic ability and was gifted in her use of pantomime.

MARIE SALLE (1707–1756)—Salle was also a student of Prevost's and was known for her dramatic ability. She performed in both Paris and London and is credited with being the first female choreographer.

MARIE CAMARGO (1710–1770)—One of Prevost's students, Camargo was a Paris Opera dancer who was known for her great technical ability, especially in performing "beats."

JEAN GEORGES NOVERRE (1727–1810)—Noverre authored *Letters on Dancing and Ballet*, which presented the concept of *ballet d' action*. In this article, choreographers were called upon to create a new type of ballet—one that had a plot and followed a logical progression, rather than being abstract.

THE ROMANTICS OF THE NINETEENTH CENTURY

CHARLES DIDELOT (1767–1837)—Didelot was a French dancer, choreographer and teacher whose choreography was characteristic of the Romantic Style. He also introduced several changes to the typically worn ballet costumes, including flesh-colored tights for women. He also employed "flying machines" in his ballets and the newly introduced pointe technique.

FILIPPO TAGLIONI (1778–1871)—An Italian dancer and choreographer, Taglioni choreographed *La Sylphide* in 1832. This ballet is said to have "begun" the Romantic Era.

CARLO BLASIS (1795–1878)—Blasis opened one of the most important dance schools in Milan (Royal Academy of Dance), where his method of teaching dance shaped much of the teaching of ballet technique. He was also an author of instructional textbooks.

MARIE TAGLIONI (1804–1884)—Daughter of Filippo Taglioni, Marie performed in many of her father's ballets. She introduced a new costume design (bare neck and shoulders, tight fitting bodice and skirt reaching just below the knee) and is known for her beautifully executed jumps and leaps. She also perfected dancing *en pointe,* and her dancing appeared effortless.

AUGUST BOURNONVILLE (1805–1879)—Once a student of the Paris Opera, Bournonville brought the Romantic ballet to his native Denmark and became director of ballet at the Royal Theatre. His dance aesthetic became a part of the Royal Danish Ballet and he worked to elevate ballet and the dance profession.

FANNY ELSSLER (1810–1884)—A dancer born in Vienna, Elssler was a rival of Marie Taglioni while they were both employed by the Paris Opera. Elssler is known for her ability to execute small, quick steps. One of Elssler's most famous roles, *Cachucha,* was a Spanish-style dance that she performed very sensuously, which led critics to call her "pagan."

JULES PERROT (1810–1892)—Co-choreographer of *Giselle* (with Jean Coralli), Perrot used movement (as opposed to pantomime) to move the storyline of the ballet along. One of his most famous ballets that was strictly movement-based was *Pas de Quatre*, choreographed in 1845 and danced by Taglioni, Grisi and two other ballerinas, Fanny Cerrito and Lucile Grahn.

CARLOTTA GRISI (1819–1899)—Grisi was an Italian ballerina who created the leading role in *Giselle,* a ballet of the Romantic Era that is still performed today.

ARTHUR SAINT-LÉON (1821–1870)—One of the last great choreographers of the Romantic era, Saint-Léon was also a dancer and violinist. He became ballet master of the Imperial Theatre in St. Petersburg in 1859 and attempted to develop a system of dance notation. The last ballet he choreographed, *Coppélia* (1870), is still performed today, although there are many different versions that are based on Saint-Léon's theme.

THE RUSSIAN INFLUENCE (1910–1930S)

MARIUS PETIPA (1818–1910)—A French-born choreographer, Petipa came to St. Petersburg in 1847. Petipa formulated "classical ballet," which stressed formal values such as symmetry and order of movements, staging, etc. Much of what we know today to be "classical" ballet directly descends from the teachings and choreography of Petipa. Some of his famous ballets are *The Sleeping Beauty* and *Swan Lake* (the latter choreographed with Lev Ivanov).

LEV IVANOV (1843–1901)—Ivanov was Petipa's assistant and also collaborated with him to develop two of today's most loved classical ballets: *Swan Lake* and *The Nutcracker*. Ivanov's choreography is best known for expressing emotion through pure classical dancing (without pantomime).

ENRICO CECCHETTI (1850–1928)—Cecchetti was an Italian whose outstanding teaching ability made him important in Russian ballet. He became the private ballet instructor for Anna Pavlova and then the ballet master for Diaghilev's Ballet Russes. The Cecchetti method of teaching is used around the world today. In 1922, the Cecchetti Society was established in England and in 1939 the Cecchetti Council of America was formed in the United States.

ALEXANDER GORSKY (1871–1924)—Gorsky began the turn away from the formality of the established classical ballet in Russia. He did away with symmetry and used character dances to embellish the storyline. He wanted to use the ideas of drama teacher and director Konstantin Stanislavsky (working from the "inside" to the outside) in his ballets. Therefore, he gave his dancers different motivations and characters on stage.

SERGE DIAGHILEV (1872–1929)—Diaghilev was the director of the Ballet Russes, which was a company made up of dancers from the Imperial Theatre of St. Petersburg (Fokine was hired as the company's first master choreographer). Diaghilev is also credited with giving **Vaslav Nijinsky** (1889–1950) his first opportunity as a choreographer. Nijinsky, known for his outstanding dancing ability, shocked audiences with his ballets *L'Apres-midi d'un Faune (The Afternoon of a Faun)* and *Le Sacre du Printemps (The Rite of Spring)*. Audiences were shocked due to the storylines which included references to sex and death, and to the unique movement style. In these ballets, Nijinsky abandoned the well-known technique of classical ballet and replaced it with stylized movements that were asymmetrical, heavy and employed both turned-in and parallel positions.

AGRIPPINA VAGANOVA (1879–1951)—Vaganova was the founder of the Soviet system of ballet education. She created a method of teaching ballet (known as the Vaganova method) that was adopted by all Soviet dance schools. Russian dancers trained in this method for many years. Today, the Vaganova method is still taught around the world.

MICHEL FOKINE (1880–1942)—Fokine followed the path that Gorsky had set up, although he believed strongly in technique. Fokine also believed that a fusion of dance, music, drama, scenery and costumes was necessary and he broke many rules of ballet to fit his aesthetic. His choreography is known as contemporary ballet.

ANNA PAVLOVA (1881–1931)—A principal dancer with Russia's Imperial Ballet and the Ballet Russes, Pavlova was known for her beautiful and dramatic dancing. One of her most famous dances was *The Dying Swan,* choreographed for her by Fokine in 1907. After she left Russia in 1911, she went to London and formed a company of English dancers (who changed their names to sound Russian). She and her company toured all over the world for many years.

BRONISLAVA NIJINSKA (1891–1972)—Nijinska was the great Nijinsky's sister and became an outstanding choreographer in her own right. Diaghilev hired her to choreograph for the Ballet Russes, and she created such ballets as *Les Noces,* in 1923, and *Les Biches,* in 1924. Her choreography was as experimental and abstract as her brother's.

LEONIDE MASSINE (1895–1979)—Massine was another choreographer hired by Diaghilev for the Ballet Russes. By 1917, with the premiere of Massine's *Parade,* the Ballet Russes had established the reputation for offering modern or contemporary ballets.

GEORGE BALANCHINE (1904–1983)—A student of the Russian Imperial School of Ballet, Balanchine toured with a small troupe of dancers until he was offered a job at the Ballet Russes, where he stayed for four years. In the year of Diaghilev's death (1929), Balanchine created one of his best-loved ballets, *The Prodigal Son,* which is still performed today. After serving as a resident choreographer for the Ballet Russes de Monte Carlo (a company created by Sergei Denham), Balanchine came to the United States in 1933 at the invitation of art patron **Lincoln Kirstein** (1907–1995). In the United States, Balanchine established the School of American Ballet and had four successive companies: The American Ballet, American Ballet Caravan, Ballet Society and the New York City Ballet (developed in 1948, it is the only one still in existence). Balanchine is best-known for his sophisticated use of music, plotless ballets and minimal costume and set design. His artistic neoclassical style has continued to keep him, even years after his death, at the forefront of today's choreographers.

BEYOND THE RUSSIAN BORDERS: BRITAIN, FRANCE AND THE UNITED STATES (1930s–1940s)

MARIE RAMBERT (1888–1982)—Rambert developed the Ballet Rambert in England in the mid-1920s. Although not a choreographer, she was a master teacher and trained many outstanding dancers. The company still exists today and is known as the Rambert Dance Company.

LUCIA CHASE (1897–1986)—An American ballerina, Chase, along with dance director **Richard Pleasant** (1906–1961), organized Ballet Theatre (now American Ballet Theatre) in New York. Beginning in 1940, Chase went on to direct the company for many years.

NINETTE DE VALOIS (1898–2001)—de Valois developed the Sadler's Wells Ballet in England in the late 1920s, which eventually became the Royal Ballet. Together with Rambert, she helped sustain the Carmargo Society, an organization developed to provide financial support for Britain's ballet companies.

FREDERICK ASHTON (1904–1988)—Ashton was a choreographer and director of the Royal Ballet, succeeding de Valois in 1963. As a student of Marie Rambert, he was encouraged to choreograph. He is best-known for the outstanding *pas de deux* sections that appear in his ballets.

SERGE LIFAR (1905–1986)—Lifar was a Russian dancer who, in 1929, became ballet master of the Paris Opera Ballet. He believed that dance should not follow the rhythm that music dictated, but should have its own rhythm. He is credited with elevating the position of the male dancer in ballet and provided several outstanding dance sequences for males in his choreography.

ANTHONY TUDOR (1908–1987)—Tudor danced in both the Ballet Rambert and Sadler's Wells (Royal Ballet) dance companies. He also choreographed for Ballet Rambert, before coming to the United States in 1940, where he joined Ballet Theatre (now the American Ballet Theatre) in New York. Tudor's choreography is known for its psychological meaning depicted through movement.

ALICIA MARKOVA (1910–2004)—An English dancer, Markova danced with Diaghilev's Ballet Russes for five years, where she changed her name to sound Russian (her birth name was Marks). She also danced with Ballet Rambert in the works of Ashton and Tudor. Markova was loved by the American dance audience as well as the Europeans.

ROLAND PETIT (b. 1924)—A French choreographer who believed the Paris Opera Ballet was too restrictive, Petit developed the *Ballet de Paris* in 1948. He is known for blending jazz and ballet techniques in his highly dramatic choreography.

RUDOLF NUREYEV (1938–1993)—Nureyev, a Russian, was a soloist with the Kirov Ballet before he defected from the Soviet Union (while the Kirov was on tour in Paris). He remained and danced in France before being hired by the Royal Ballet. Here, he was partnered with ballerina **Margot Fonteyn** (1919–1991), who was a British dancer. Their partnership is among the best-known and loved in the ballet world. Together they danced in many famous ballets and are well-known for their work in *Romeo and Juliet*, choreographed by Kenneth MacMillan.

INTO THE PRESENT

AGNES DE MILLE (1905–1993)—An American dancer trained in ballet, de Mille choreographed on such companies as the Ballet Russes de Monte Carlo and the American Ballet Theatre. She is also known for her choreography of musical theatre productions such as *Oklahoma,* in 1943, and *Carousel,* in 1945.

CATHERINE LITTLEFIELD (1908–1951)—Littlefield was the founder of the Littlefield Ballet, later to be known as the Philadelphia Ballet. She is credited with presenting the first full-length American production of *The Sleeping Beauty.* She also choreographed for ice skaters and presented ballet on ice in a 1940s production entitled *It Happens on Ice.*

JEROME ROBBINS (1918–1998)—An American dancer and choreographer, Robbins performed with the Ballet Theatre for eight years. He has choreographed on several ballet companies, particularly New York City Ballet, of which he was associate artistic director from 1949 to 1963. He also co-directed New York City Ballet with Peter Martins in the 1980s, until the end of the 1990–1991 season. Robbins is also known for his musical theatre choreography, such as *West Side Story* (1961).

MAURICE BÉJART (b. 1927)—Béjart, from France, danced with many leading European companies. His debut as a choreographer was in 1954. In 1959, he was appointed director of the *Theatre Royal de la Monnaie* in Brussels, Belgium, where he stayed until 1988. Béjart's choreography is referred to as contemporary, sexy and dramatic.

YURI GRIGOROVICH (b. 1927)—A Russian, Grigorovich danced with the Kirov and eventually became a prolific choreographer. In 1964, he became chief choreographer of the Bolshoi Ballet, where he is credited with the creation of characterization through dance.

KENNETH MACMILLAN (1929–1992)—Macmillan was a Scottish dancer and choreographer who succeeded Frederik Ashton as artistic director of the Royal Ballet. He is known for creating ballets that employed large casts and lavish costumes.

ROBERT JOFFREY (1930–1988)—An American ballet dancer and choreographer, Joffrey established the Joffrey Ballet in 1954. This company is primarily known for dancing contemporary works by leading choreographers such as Joffrey and Alvin Ailey. **GERALD ARPINO** (b. 1928) also choreographed for the company and served as assistant director. After Joffrey's death, Arpino took over artistic directorship of the company.

ARTHUR MITCHELL (b. 1934)—Previously a dancer with New York City Ballet, Mitchell wanted to develop a company where African-American dancers could perform in classical ballets. In 1972, he established Dance Theatre of Harlem, which today performs around the world.

NATALIA MAKAROVA (b. 1940)—A Russian dancer who defected to the United States, Makarova is one of today's most well-known ballerinas.

ELIOT FELD (b. 1942)—Previously a dancer with American Ballet Theatre, Feld established the Feld Ballet in 1974, later called Ballet Tech, which performed contemporary ballets that were described as fast-paced and sexy. Although Ballet Tech disbanded in 2003, Feld still choreographs and presents concerts.

HELGI TOMASSON (b. 1942)—Tomasson has been the artistic director of the San Francisco Ballet since 1985. Originally from Iceland, Tomasson studied at the School of American Ballet in New York in the early 1960s, and joined the Joffrey Ballet in 1962. Today, the San Francisco Ballet is an internationally known company, whose dancers are recognized for their powerful technique and dramatic performance ability.

PETER MARTINS (b. 1946)—A Danish dancer and choreographer who performed with New York City Ballet for many years, Martins is now the artistic director of New York City Ballet. He has been in this role since 1983 and also choreographs for the company.

JIRI KYLIAN (b. 1947)—Kylian is the artistic director of the Netherlands Dance Theatre, whose works are a combination of modern dance and ballet. Kylian's works are dramatic and usually fast-paced and powerful.

MIKHAIL BARYSHNIKOV (b. 1948)—A Russian dancer with the Kirov Ballet, Baryshnikov defected while on a tour in Canada in 1974. After several guest appearances with different companies, Baryshnikov went to American Ballet Theatre where he danced for several years. He also served as artistic director of the company. Today, Baryshnikov is involved in several projects, including dancing with the White Oak Dance Project, which he co-founded in 1990 with choreographer Mark Morris.

ALEXANDER GODUNOV (1950–1995)—A principal dancer with the Bolshoi Ballet, Godunov defected from the Soviet Union to the West in 1979. He became a principal dancer with American Ballet Theatre, and performed with them until 1982. He left his dance career for a career in movies, with one of his most popular roles being that of an Amish farmer in the movie *Witness*.

KAROLE ARMITAGE (b. 1954)—Although trained in ballet, Armitage joined the modern Cunningham Dance Company in 1975. After she left the Cunningham Company, she began, in the late 1970s, to create ballets that have been referred to as "punk-rock" ballets, because of their use of punk-rock music, costumes, hair styles and makeup. She is still an active choreographer today.

MATTHEW BOURNE (b. 1960)—Bourne, from London, is the former Artistic Director of Adventures in Motion Pictures, and the current Artistic Director of New Adventures. In 1995, he choreographed a critically acclaimed version of *Swan Lake* in which all of the swans are men. This production has been called groundbreaking and has won a record number of awards, including two Tony awards for Choreography and Direction. In 2004, Bourne choreographed and co-directed Disney's *Mary Poppins*. One of his latest projects is a stage version of *Edward Scissorhands* (2005).

CHRISTOPHER WHEELDON (b. 1973)—Wheeldon was born in England and began his ballet training when he was 8 years old. In 1991 he danced with the Royal Ballet, and in 1993 he was invited to join New York City Ballet. In 2001, Wheeldon was named Resident Choreographer of New York City Ballet.

Early History of Dance

A BASIC UNDERSTANDING OF DANCE

Dance is around us everywhere, from children skipping and singing on the playground, to classes on ballroom or salsa dancing, to social dancing at parties and clubs, to amateur and professional dances in the theatre. Dance is a beautiful art, and it is found today in a wide variety of forms.

This text attempts to cover the history of dance from its primitive origins to the present day. But in order to discuss dance knowledgeably and to begin to have an appreciation for it, certain basic terminology must be understood.

In observing a dance performance, several components should be considered including the choreography, the ability of the dancers to perform that choreography, the costumes and make-up, the lighting, the set or scenery, and the music.

The choreographer is the person who creates the dance. Choreographers use the body as their medium to express their creative ideas. Sometimes a choreographer tells a story through dance. Other times, the dance is "abstract" or plotless, created as "art for art's sake." In discussing the choreography of a dance, it is important to try to appreciate the message the choreographer is trying to convey. In reviewing the choreography, one might discuss the different genres of dance. Is the choreography that of a classical ballet, perhaps on point and with a traditional story being told? Or is it modern, done in bare feet? We can discuss the choreography of a musical theatre piece being performed on Broadway, or that of a tap dance routine.

Next, consider the performance of the dancers themselves. Are they well-trained professionals, or are they amateurs? How many dancers are used in the piece, and how well prepared are they for their roles? Consider the look of the piece as performed by the dancers.

THE PRIMITIVE PERIOD: TO 3000 B.C.

Dance is certainly one of the earliest forms of art. Painters need brushes and paint to produce their art, and musicians need instruments of some form. But dancers use their bodies as their medium. Through dance, man has been able to communicate his thoughts and feelings.

Historically, dance was used as a method of communication with the gods. Dance rituals were performed to worship or to appease the gods. Several types of early religious dances can be noted. Early man performed dances of imitation in which they patterned their movement around objects in nature which they observed. Often these dances involved imitation of animals. For example, Native American dancers are seen to perform a dance in which they imitate the flight of an eagle. Their movements imitate the bird's actions by having arms spread apart as in flight and by mimicking the soaring pattern the eagle makes. Their dress, too, imitates that of a bird by incorporating the feathers along the sleeves of their costumes. Dances of imitation might also include imitating the movements of the wind, or of water or of the swaying of trees or of other movement found in nature.

Commemorative dances were often performed by an entire community to mark an important event. A dance ritual might be performed at a birth to ensure a healthy life for the child. A commemorative dance could be performed on the occasion of a wedding, or upon a death to ask for a peaceful transition for the spirit.

Medicine dances were performed to restore the health of an individual by warding off evil spirits or by pleasing a certain god or goddess. They were also used to protect an individual, family or community from danger or disease,

Dances for spiritual connection were a form of prayer, used to establish a connection with the gods or spirits. Dances of spiritual connection might have been done for a good harvest or a successful hunting expedition.

The movements for these dances were very basic and natural. They were based on the natural rhythms of the body such as the beating of the heart or breathing. Simple movements such as hopping, running, skipping, stomping and swaying were used.

Early "music" would have been very natural and basic as well. Clapping, humming, singing and shouting might have set the tempo for these dances. As man began to develop early percussion instruments, the tapping of sticks and the introduction of drums would add rhythm.

Because these dances were rituals, they were not spontaneous. Father to son or mother to daughter, these dances were passed down from generation to generation.

ANCIENT PERIOD 3000 B.C. TO 400 A.D.

In this period, we begin to see a conscious element of the aesthetic. The Greeks incorporated dance into their theatre. Poetry, theatre and dance were important aspects of life. Dance was not done as a ritual, but as a pleasing form of art and entertainment.

In India, there is a long tradition of dance. From 500–300 B.C., a dance called Bharata Natyam was developed. Bharata Natyam was a temple dance that was graceful and required great skill. It is a form of prayer that uses exact hand, eye and other body movements. The feet are moved quickly, and bells and other ornaments enhance the dance. It is still practiced today.

THE MEDIEVAL PERIOD 400 A.D. TO 1400 A.D.

In the Medieval era, dance was not celebrated as a form of entertainment. The church was influential in dictating what happened in society, and dance was considered a frivolity. The emphasis at the time was on the purity of the soul, and matters of the body were not celebrated. The outbreak of the Black (bubonic) Plague led to a focus on death. The danse macabre, or dance of death, became an obsession of the era as society was surrounded by the immensity of the death at the time. The figure of the Grim Reaper, with an hour glass in one hand to remind one of the finite time in the world and the scythe in the other hand to tell of the nearness of death, would be seen as a reminder that death was at hand.

Colloquial dance, however, continued as people performed dances such as the Maypole dance. Here, a pole was decorated with ribbons, and young men and women would dance and weave the streamers around the pole.

RENAISSANCE/LOUIS XIV

THE RENAISSANCE PERIOD 1400-1700 A.D.

The Renaissance, or a period of "rebirth," was a direct response to the oppressive times of the Dark and Middle Ages. There was a renewed interest in scholarship and the art of the classical world of Greece and Rome. The arts including painting, sculpture, music, literature, poetry and dance were celebrated and patronized by the wealthy nobility and by the rising merchant class.

Dance was important as an art form in this period, and it was critical in establishing social status. Court ballets were developed at this time, and social dance was considered an essential element in the training and education of the nobility. In fact, many noblemen retained the services of a "Dance Master" to train them in the newly important dance steps so that they might find favor at court.

These court dances were done in elaborate dress, including heavy long gowns, wigs and headdresses. Consequently, much of the dancing involved posing or simply gliding. Generally, dances were divided into two categories. In Basse Danse, which is "low dance" in French, the feet stayed on or very close to the floor. In Haute Danse ("high dance"), there were higher movements such as jumps or skips.

Some of the most prominent dances of the period were the Pavane, the Galliard, the Allemande, the Courante, the Sarabande, the Gigue, and the Minuet.

Pavane—This dance's name is probably derived from the Italian and Spanish words for peacock as the women swept their trains as a peacock sweeps his tail. It was a Basse Danse involving dignified and slow steps.

Galliard—A Haute Danse, the Galliard was lively and involved leaping and kicking. This high-spirited dance usually followed the Pavane.

Allemande—Of German origin, this dance was simple and slow. It required the dancers to keep their hands joined together.

Courante—"Running dance" in French, began as a lively dance, but evolved into a more slow and solemn dance.

Gigue—A Haute Danse, this spirited dance evolved into what we now call the "jig." It was usually done to the music of a fiddle.

Minuet—From the French for "small steps," this dance involved sweeping movements and curtsies and bows.

EARLY BALLET

In its early form, ballet was quite different from what we now think of as ballet. Catherine de Medici (1519–1589) is considered by many to be the "mother of dance." From a prominent family in Florence, Italy, Catherine de Medici married into the royal family of Henri, Duc d'Orleans of France. She brought with her from Italy her head dancing master, Balthasar de Beaujoyeux. In 1581, he created what is considered to be the first court ballet, the Ballet Comique de La Reine. This "court ballet" was a "spectacle" and was performed over a period of about five or more hours. The noble men and women were the performers, and elaborate costumes were used. This production was extremely expensive. The dancers were placed in poses and performed elaborate patterns in their heavy costumes. The ballet, which included stories from the Old Testament and from Greek and Roman mythology, incorporated dance, original music, and poetry. The sets were very elaborate.

LOUIS XIV

Louis XIV, who ruled France from 1643–1715, was one of the greatest patrons of dance. He took daily lessons from his dancing master Pierre Beauchamps, and during his reign, a nobleman's status at court was largely determined by his dancing skills. Louis XIV loved to participate in the performances, and he is considered to be one of the first "stars" of the ballet world. He received his name, "the Sun King," from his role of that name in the Ballet Royal de la Nuit. Louis XIV performed as the lead dancer in many ballets at the Louvre, Versailles, and Fountainbleau. Only when he got older and began to gain weight did he begin to lose his interest in these lead roles. He remained passionate about dance and in 1661 established the Royal Academy of Dance under the direction of the Italian born Jean-Baptiste Lully. Pierre Beauchamps, Louis' dancing master also became involved at the Royal Academy. Beauchamps made a significant contribution to ballet history by codifying the five positions of the foot. These positions are still used today. He also encouraged the use of the "turned out" position. The Royal Academy of Ballet served as a training ground for professional dancers. During this period we see a shift from the dances being performed by nobility to those performed by professionals (the rise of the professional dancer). There was also a shift from Court ballet performed in a ballroom setting to the performances occurring in a theater setting. Specifically, it is during this period when we see the development of the *proscenium stage*, which is a stage at one end of a hall or theater. The performers are elevated and separated from the audience by a proscenium arch. As opposed to the court ballet where the audience was seated all around the performers, the audience now only sees the front of the stage and the performers. This format made the turned out position of the dancers important.

JEAN GEORGE NOVERRE

Ballet saw great reform under Jean George Noverre (1727–1810). Until Noverre, ballet had been a collection of short dances that were not tied together by plot. Noverre's writings on the ballet d'action were published in his book *Letters on Dancing and Ballet* (1760). He proposed several changes:

1. Balletic movements should be technically brilliant and should move the audience emotionally.
2. The plots of the ballets should be unified in design, with understandable stories that are centered around the main theme.
3. There should be unity in costumes, music, scenery, and plot.
4. Pantomime needed to be made more simple (a system of hand gestures used instead of words).

THE RISE OF THE FEMALE STARS OF BALLET

Women began to emerge as the stars of ballet with the rise of professional dance training. Marie Anne de Camargo (1710–1770) was one of the most outstanding French dancers of her time. Camargo was a technician who longed for the freedom of movement allowed male dancers. She raised her skirt hems permitting more aerial work and beats of the legs. She also developed soft slippers which eventually lead to the development of the modern ballet slipper.

Another star of the era was Marie Sallé. Her style differed from the quick movements of Camargo. She sought a more natural movement that portrayed realism. In her costumes, she favored soft draping modeled after Greek sculpture.

THE ROMANTIC PERIOD

The French Revolution caused a revolution in dance too. During this period, the ordinary citizen was glorified rather than royalty. In many ballets, the presence of the supernatural was depicted. Ballerinas began to dance on the tips of their toes to enhance the sensation of skimming across the stage like sylphs or ghosts. The heavy costumes of the court dancers were replaced with the lightweight skirt fabrics called tulle. Ballets were performed in two acts. The first act was usually set in a village or "civilized" setting. In contrast, the second act was usually set in nature, perhaps in a moor or woods setting. This helped show the contrast of civilization versus nature or even the supernatural. The appearance of the fairy-like sylphs in "La Sylphide" is an example of these supernatural beings.

Marie Taglioni (1804–1884) and Fanny Essler (1810–1884) became rivals. Taglioni excelled in ballets that emphasized her delicacy and lightness. The ballet *La Sylphide* was created for her in 1832 by her father Filippo Taglioni. Her style was very feminine and fragile. This ballet was the first to be performed all on pointe. Essler was famous for her passionate dancing. Her style was "earthy" and was even described as pagan. She excelled in folk dancing and went on tour in America.

Giselle (1841) was choreographed by Jules Perrot and became a very popular romantic ballet. The original ballet is set in a village in Germany. The second act is set in the mystical and moonlit land of the Wilis, the spirits of brides who died before their wedding day. A contemporary version of this ballet, entitled *Creole Giselle* and staged by Arthur Mitchell for the Dance Theater of Harlem, is set in the swamps of Louisiana. Mitchell danced with the New York City Ballet and was the first black dancer to rise to the level of principle in a major American ballet company.

The Pas de Quatre was a ballet divertissement choreographed by Jules Perrot premiering in 1845. It brought together the four greatest ballet dancers of the day: Marie Taglioni, the Italian ballerinas Carlotta Grisi (1821–1899) and Fanny Cerrito (1821–1899), and the Danish dancer Lucille Grahn (1821–1907). Perrot emphasized each dancers' skills in this plotless ballet, although there were rivalries in this group as well. In costuming, we see the development of the romantic length tutu, made of the net fabric tulle and which is cut to calf-length. "Ballet blanc" is the focus with the female dancers dressed in white.

Gradually, there was a decline in interest in these ballets that emphasized the female stars, and great male dancers began to make the next changes in ballet.

THE CLASSICAL ERA

A shift in the center of ballet activity from France to Russia occurred during the middle of the 19th century. This period was a golden age for ballet in Russia. Ballet technique took a giant step forward. Aerial work, turns and leg beats, and pointe work all increased in skill and perfection. The tutu, a short skirt, was also created. Marius Petipa (1818–1910) the "father of the classical ballet" arrived in Russia in 1847 to dance at the Imperial Theater. This theater later became known as the Maryinsky Theater. Petipa became a ballet master of the theater in 1858 and by 1870 was in sole control. Under his direction, Russia became the leading country for ballet. He became the most famous choreographer in the ballet world. Some of his most famous ballets include: *The Sleeping Beauty* (1890), *Don Quixote* (1869), *Cinderella* (1893), *The Nutcracker* (1892), and *Swan Lak*e (1895). Lev Ivanov co-choreographed *Nutcracker* and *Swan Lake*. *The Nutcracker* has become the most popular ballet to see during the Christmas season. Petipa collaborated with the composer Peter Tchaikovsky to create the music for many of his ballets. Tchaikovsky composed the music for *Sleeping Beauty, The Nutcracker,* and *Swan Lake*. Because he understood gesture, pantomime, and the rhythm of the dancing body, he could write music perfectly for the choreographer and the dancer.

These classical ballets rely heavily on the plot and often tell fairytale stories. The development of the classical tutu allows the full leg of the ballerinas to be seen. In classical ballets, ballerinas wear pointe shoes. The men are usually costumed in tunics and tights, and all of the costumes are very elaborate. The sets too were very ornate.

In classical ballet, we find the division of dancers into categories. The principals are the lead dancers. The prima ballerina is the lead female dancer. The premier danseur is the highest ranking male dancer. Next are the soloists who perform character roles or solo dances. Finally, we have the corps de ballet, the chorus or "body" of dancers who perform together as a group. The corps de ballet may serve in dancing roles, but often in classical ballets they serve as background by way of maintaining a pose behind the action of the principle or soloist.

Classical ballets highlight the grand pas de deux, or step for two. It begins with an adagio, or slow duet, performed by the male and female leads. The male dancer performs a solo variation next, which is usually quite athletic. Next, the female lead performs her solo variation. This variation is usually intricate and difficult. The pair then come together for the coda, the final movement. This movement is an energetic partnering between the two.

Pantomime is the use of hand motions to tell a story and is heavily used in classical ballet.

CONTEMPORARY BALLET

Contemporary Ballet was developed in Russia under the guidance of Serge Diaghilev (1872–1929). Diaghilev was a dynamic and creative force who envisioned a new era in dance. Though he was neither a dancer nor a choreographer, he was a producer who was able to draw together highly talented dancers and choreographers. Diaghilev's company, the Ballet Russes, was founded in 1909, and one of its most famous choreographers was Michel Fokine (1880–1947). Fokine was a brilliant dancer who partnered with the famous ballerina Anna Pavlova (1881–1931). Fokine achieved great success as a choreographer. Some of his famous works include: *Firebird* (1910), *Le Spectre de la Rose* (1911), and *Petrouchka* (1911). Some of his ideas for change included using dance movement rather than pantomime to develop the dramatic action. He also placed more importance on the roles of the corps de ballet.

In 1912, Diaghilev replaced Fokine as choreographer with the famous dancer Vaslav Nijinsky (1889–1950). Nijinsky, whose ballet career extended only over a nine year period, is purported to be one of the greatest male dancers of all time. As a dancer, Nijinsky excelled in jumping and turning. He often played exotic roles and was a tremendously popular star of his day. As a choreographer, his works were quite shocking in their storylines of death and sex. His *L'Apres-midi d'un Faune* (the *Afternoon of a Faun*, 1912) was overtly sexual in nature and is very different in terms of choreography by the use of two dimensional and parallel leg movements. Ultimately, Nijinsky's career ended tragically as he was diagnosed as mentally ill and was confined to a sanatorium until his death.

The Ballet Ruses toured internationally, but in 1923 Diaghilev contracted for the company to become the official ballet of Monte Carlo in the principality of Monaco. The name was changed to Les Ballets Russes de Monte Carlo. The company ultimately dissolved at Diaghilev's death in 1929. Many of the dancers and choreographers had left before this time.

There are similarities between classical and contemporary ballets, such as the use of a common vocabulary for the movements. The rejection of pantomime by contemporary choreographers is a difference. Classical ballet music is usually melodious whereas contemporary ballet might use music that is more abstract or atonal. One composer who is often associated with the contemporary period is Igor

Stravinsky (1882–1971). His compositions include: *The Firebird* (1910), *Petrouchka* (1911), and *Rite of Spring* (1913).

DANCE IN AMERICA

George Balanchine (1904–1983) was born in St Petersburg, Russia and entered the famous Imperial School of Ballet at the age of 10. Though accomplished as a dancer, it is as a choreographer that Balanchine is widely known. He was a part of Diaghilev's choreographic team for the Ballet Russes. While choreographing for the Ballet Russes, Balanchine met the composer Igor Stravinsky. They became lifelong collaborators.

Balanchine was invited by Lincoln Kirstein (1907–1995), a wealthy American, to come to the United States, and he did so in 1933. Together they laid the foundation for the future of American ballet. Balanchine is regarded as one of ballet's greatest visionaries, and he and Kirstein founded the New York City Ballet, one of the most highly regarded dance companies in the world. With the arrival of Balanchine in America, we see a shift in focus on dance away from Russia to the innovative "neoclassical" style that Balanchine developed in America.

A brief list of Balanchine's ballets (he created more than 200) includes: *Apollo* (1928), *The Prodigal Son* (1929), *Mozartiana* (1933), *Seranade* (1934), *The Four Temperaments* (1946), *Allegro Brillante* (1956), *Agon* (1957), *Stars and Stripes* (1958), *Jewels* (1967), *Who Cares?* (1970), *Violin Concerto* (1972), and others.

Balanchine also choreographed for Broadway musicals including *On Your Toes* (1936), and *The Boys from Syracuse* (1938), as well as for TV and movies.

Modern Dance

INTRODUCTION

This chapter explores the genres of modern dance, post-modern dance and dance-theatre from the beginning to the present day. Although these genres are closely related in aesthetic and artistic principles, they also have unique and distinct characteristics. Today, these three genres are widely recognized, and are studied and performed throughout the world.

MODERN DANCE: THE BEGINNING

In comparison to ballet, modern dance is a relatively new dance form (beginning in the late 1800s and early 1900s), evolving as a direct revolt against what was perceived as the "restrictions" of ballet. Many dance historians credit Isadora Duncan (1877–1927, see Figure 3.1), with being the first dancer to present "modern dancing" to the public, although performers such as Loie Fuller (1862–1928, see Figure 3.2) and Maud Allan (1883–1956, see "Major Figures in Modern Dance") certainly did present to audiences dancing that was new and different.

Duncan's reasons for moving and creating, however, were different from those of Fuller's and Allan's. After years of ballet training, Duncan began to feel that the pointe shoes and the costumes that ballerinas wore were too confining, as was the ballet vocabulary. She decided to leave her technical training and began to dance in a way that seemed to her to be more natural. She was inspired by the movements of the trees, the ocean and by all of nature. Duncan developed a technique that used movements such as hopping, running, swaying and skipping; movements that seemed natural and expressive to her. The solar plexus, in the center of the body, was the area from which all movement was generated. She was inspired by the history of the Greeks and she danced barefoot and in sheer tunics similar to the Greek style. She felt that these tunics did not restrict her movements and that they also showed the beauty of the female body. Duncan, known to many in America as a rebel, found fame (and an enthusiastic audience) in several parts of Europe and Russia, from 1904–1927. While she was in Russia, many believe that Duncan's "new" dance form inspired many of the contemporary ballet cho-

In comparison to ballet, modern dance is a relatively new dance form, evolving as a direct revolt against what was perceived as the "restrictions" of ballet.

Figure 3.1
Isadora Duncan. Jerome Robbins Dance Division, The New York Public Library for the Performing Arts, Astor, Lenox and Tilden Foundations.

reographers, such as Michel Fokine. Eventually, the American audiences accepted her and she paved the way for all of the modern dancers and choreographers who were to follow.

Duncan danced to music composed by Beethoven, Schubert and Wagner, among others, but had a particular love for music by Chopin. Many of her dances clearly portrayed her love and passion for moving. However, in 1913, Duncan's two children were killed in a tragic car accident. This event led her to create a dance, entitled *Mother*, which depicted a sorrowful and broken figure. Eventually, Duncan opened a school of dance. Six of her students, referred to by dance critics as the "Isadorables," were all adopted by Isadora and took the Duncan last name. Three of these students, Irma, Ana and Maria Theresa, were the people responsible

Figure 3.2
Loie Fuller, photo by
Falk. Jerome Robbins
Dance Division, The
New York Public
Library for the
Performing Arts,
Astor, Lenox and
Tilden Foundations.

for teaching the Duncan technique after Isadora's death. Today, there are individuals and dance companies who are dedicated to keeping the Duncan legacy alive.

Many modern dance choreographers emerged after Isadora Duncan, each contributing their own aesthetic and philosophical opinions to the dance world, as well as their own "technique" or "style" of dance. For example, Ruth St. Denis (1878–1968, see Figure 3.3) and Ted Shawn (1891–1972) were two dancers who married and formed a school (in 1915) that they called Denishawn. St. Denis and Shawn were greatly influenced by different cultures, particularly of the Asian countries. Though the dances they performed were not authentic, Denishawn brought a view

Figure 3.3
Ruth St. Denis.
Jerome Robbins
Dance Division,
The New York
Public Library
for the Perform-
ing Arts, Astor,
Lenox and Tilden
Foundations.

of the dance of other countries to the American audience. The main educational purpose of the Denishawn school, however, was to educate the "total" dancer—meaning the body, mind and spirit.

St. Denis and Shawn developed a company using pupils from the school. They performed on the vaudeville circuit, as well as in other theatres across the country. They eventually toured several Asian countries, where they not only performed but also studied the dances of the countries that they were so fond of depicting. Three major dance figures to come out of the Denishawn School were Martha Graham, Doris Humphrey and Charles Weidman. These three artists, sometimes referred to as the "pioneers" of modern dance, had a major impact on the dance world. Although most ballets can be easily divided into the categories of classical or contemporary, many different "techniques" or "styles" can be categorized under the heading of modern dance (refer to "Major Figures in Modern Dance" for an overview of different dancers who created specific techniques).

Dancer and choreographer Martha Graham (1894–1990, see Figure 3.4) developed a technique that was based on the idea of "contracting" and "releasing" through the center of the body. These specific movements can be seen throughout her dances and also in the exercises of a modern dance class taught by a "Graham" teacher. Many other dancers and choreographers were and are recognized for creating a specific technique or style of dance. Erick Hawkins (1909–1994), a dancer in Graham's company for many years, developed a technique that stressed the ease and free flow of movement. Dancers studying his technique learn to perform movements using the minimum amount of muscular energy necessary, instead focusing more on the movements of the bones and skeleton.

Figure 3.4
Martha Graham in *Legend of Judith.* Jerome Robbins Dance Division, The New York Public Library for the Performing Arts, Astor, Lenox and Tilden Foundations.

On the other hand, Doris Humphrey (1895–1958) and Charles Weidman (1901–1975) developed a technique that was built around the premise of "fall and recovery." Dancers studying this technique learned to be proficient in balancing and ceding to the pull of gravity. José Limon (1908–1972), a student of Doris Humphrey, further developed (using many of the principles of his teacher) a technique that develops balance, speed and control.

Thousands of dancers have trained in the modern dance genre since the days of Isadora Duncan. Today, a dancer can choose to study one specific technique, or several. Many teachers today choose to teach an eclectic type of dance technique, drawing concepts from the more formalized and recognized styles. Unfortunately, several teachers teach a "watered-down" version of a particular technique and their students do not learn the appropriate methods of the original style. Since the years are passing and we are getting further away from the original pioneers and their first students, it is now up to those people who are schooled in the specific techniques to keep them alive and pure. Although many great artists have died, their dances live on in their still-active companies such as the Martha Graham Dance Company, Erick Hawkins Dance Company and the José Limon Dance Company.

Modern dancers and choreographers were concerned not only with developing different styles of moving, but also with creating different themes and ideas to dance about. In comparison to the fairy-tales of classical ballets, modern dance choreographers were (and are) more concerned with, among other things, the human condition and real-life situations and emotions. For example, Martha Graham created dances that dealt with psychological issues. She used themes relating to American life, the American Indian and Greek mythology to initiate her choreography. One famous dance she choreographed, entitled *Appalachian Spring* (1944), celebrates traditional domestic values by depicting the life of a young married couple. In contrast, Graham also created *Cave of the Heart* (1946), where she portrayed the jealous and bitter Medea. Nevertheless, all Graham dances utilize her strong technique, which demonstrates intense muscular energy and control, sharp angles and contraction and release of the center of the body.

Doris Humphrey and Charles Weidman (see Figure 3.5), although both part of the same company (the Humphrey-Weidman Dance Company), had different interests when it came to creating dances. Humphrey was interested in group dynamics and choreographed many dances that highlighted the group instead of soloists. She also had a strong connection to the music and worked with a technique called "music visualization," which Ruth St. Denis had introduced to her. Music visualization is a way to "see" the music through the dance, sometimes having the dancers follow specific instruments or rhythmic patterns. Humphrey also choreographed dances that were danced in silence. In this way, she greatly influenced how the dancers performed the movement, stressing specific rhythms, dynamics and the use of breath phrasing. Her dance entitled *Water Study* (1928) is a perfect example of a dance that is not bound to music, but is truly musical, simply because of the unique way in which the dance is choreographed. All sixteen dancers who originally performed the dance had to be very much in tune with each other in order to perform the movements in correct sequence and at the right time. Weidman, although he held the same values and beliefs as his partner, was also interested in comedy in dance. Whereas Humphrey's dances were dramatic and

In comparison to the fairy-tales of classical ballets, modern dance choreographers were (and are) more concerned with, among other things, the human condition and real-life situations and emotions.

Figure 3.5
Doris Humphrey and
Charles Weidman.
Jerome Robbins
Dance Division, The
New York Public
Library for the Per-
forming Arts, Astor,
Lenox and Tilden
Foundations.

emotional, such as *The Shakers* (1931), a dance about members of a religious sect,
Weidman's dances were often comic in nature. He used a technique he called "ki-
netic pantomime," in which music, and movement performed in silence, would
alternate. He did, however, choreograph many serious and dramatic dances. *Lynch
Town* (1935) was a dance that depicted the evil and sadistic behavior of a crowd
present at a lynching.

Anna Sokolow (1912–2000, see Figure 3.6), a former Graham dancer, created
dances that reflected the reality of her time. In 1955, Sokolow created *Rooms*,

Figure 3.6
Anna Sokolow.
Isadora Bennett
Collection, Jerome
Robbins Dance Divi-
sion, The New York
Public Library for the
Performing Arts,
Astor, Lenox and
Tilden Foundations.

which depicted life in the inner-city, showing people in their most vulnerable and depressed states. This depiction was a realistic and profound one in the 1950s and remains pertinent today. Not all modern dance choreography, however, has a theme, storyline, or conveys an emotion, as evidenced in the following discussion of post-modern choreographers.

Since the term "modern dance" has meant so many things to so many people, can it be clearly defined? Dance critic Selma Jeanne Cohen wrote:

> *The modern dance is a point of view, an attitude toward the function of art in the contemporary world. As the world changes, the modern dance will change, for the symbols will again—as they become acceptable—lose their power to evoke the hidden realities. They will again have to be recharged, revitalized; even demolished and recreated anew in order to serve their function. Unless this happens, the modern dance is not modern—it is dead.[1]*

Not all modern dance choreography has a theme, storyline, or conveys an emotion.

This quote provides a powerful message for all dancers and dance audiences, but particularly for choreographers; the dance is modern if it is "recreated anew." Regardless of the themes or issues that modern dance choreographers choose to deal with, one role of the modern dance artist is to provide for the audience a view into life's realities, complexities and experiences.

POST-MODERN DANCE

In the 1950s, dancers and choreographers began to feel restricted by the teachings of their predecessors. Until this time, most dance techniques were rigorous, requiring dancers to study and train for many years in order to become proficient at their art. As Isadora Duncan had revolted against ballet, this generation of dancers wanted to take their choreography in a different direction than their teachers. These new choreographers were not concerned with the dramatic and the realistic, as many of their predecessors had been, but believed that other factors were more important to include in their choreography. One of these factors, for example, was to reflect *movement*, rather than the storyline, as the primary focus of the dance. Because of this philosophy, the works of these choreographers, for the most part, came to be known as "abstract." These people were also commonly referred to as being part of the "avant garde," meaning that they were leaders in a new and unconventional movement—specifically, the post-modern movement.

Merce Cunningham (b. 1919, see Figure 3.7) was the first choreographer to emerge from using traditional modern dance choreographic methods and developed a new style of choreography. Unlike his predecessors, Cunningham did not believe that a dance had to possess a theme or storyline. His concept of dance revolved around the idea of "movement for movement's sake." In other words, *movement* should be the primary focus in the dance and should not be executed in order to depict a story to the audience. According to writer Sally Banes, Cunningham's philosophy holds the following beliefs:

> *. . . any movement can be material for a dance; any procedure can be followed and used as a compositional method; any part of the body can be used; music, costumes, set design, lighting and the movements all have their own identity and simply occur in the same place at the same time; any dancer in the company can be a soloist; a dance can be performed in any space; and a dance can be about anything, but it is primarily about the human body moving.[2]*

Figure 3.7
Merce Cunningham.
Jerome Robbins
Dance Division, The
New York Public
Library for the Per-
forming Arts, Astor,
Lenox and Tilden
Foundations.

Cunningham, who refers to his concerts as "events," often uses "chance" and "indeterminacy" methods in his choreography. These methods are tools that Cunningham believes helps him to break old habits and to create new and exciting moments in his dances. For example, chance methods might be used to determine specific movement order, phrase order, dancer's directions and floor patterns on stage, or in what order the sections of a dance will be. In 1953, Cunningham created a dance called *Suite by Chance*, in which a toss of a coin determined different aspects of spatial designs, timing and order of movement sequences. Indeterminacy, a wholly different concept, is a method in which the elements of the dance can change from performance to performance. In *Field Dances,* created in 1963, the dancers were permitted to take the movements that they were previously given and perform them in different ways, such as repeating a section, reversing a section, etc. Therefore, using indeterminacy methods, a dance that is performed a certain way one night might not be performed the same way the next.

Cunningham also collaborated with several avant garde musicians, including David Tudor, Toshi Ichiyanagi and Gordon Mumma. His most noted collaborations were with the composer John Cage (1912–1992), who held the same philosophical beliefs as Cunningham and also used chance and indeterminacy methods in his compositions. Contemporary visual artists such as Andy Warhol, Jasper Johns and Robert Rauschenberg created set and costume designs for several of Cunningham's works.

Alwin Nikolais (1912–1993), another choreographer who rebelled against the traditional methods of choreographing, did not feel that the "self" always had to be the main focus on stage. Dancers appearing in his works were often presented in costumes that made them appear more as objects than humans (see Figure 3.8). For example, Nikolais choreographed a dance entitled *Sanctum* (1964), in which the dancers appear (in one section) totally encased in bags made of material. The dancers inside manipulate the bags. The visual effect was unlike anything many dance audiences had ever seen. Nikolais is also known for integrating dance, music and design. He often created his own sound scores, costumes, props and lighting designs for his dances.

Nikolais' works were primarily abstract, and it was the *motion*, not the *emotion* that he was concerned with. In his early days as a choreographer, many dance critics accused him of dehumanizing the dancers in his works, but Nikolais did not perceive his work in this way. He believed that he was presenting to the audience a view of another experience, one that was not concerned with human feelings and emotions, but with the beauty and power of movement.

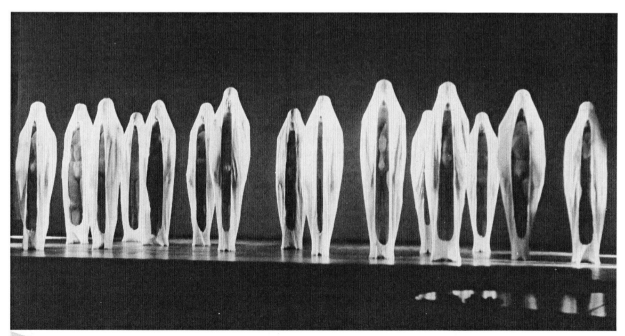

Figure 3.8
Alwin Nikolais Dance Company in "Sanctum." Jerome Robbins Dance Division, The New York Public Library for the Performing Arts, Astor, Lenox and Tilden Foundations.

Paul Taylor (b. 1930, see Figure 3.9) is another choreographer who is credited with influencing the post-modern movement. Taylor danced with both Graham and Cunningham, but went on to develop his own personal aesthetic. His earlier works utilized untraditional music, often referred to as sound scores, as well as pedestrian movements. In 1957, Taylor stood motionless for an entire "dance." In the newspaper review of the dance, the critic responded by leaving a blank space in the review column. Taylor, however, did go on to develop a very athletic and dynamic dance vocabulary. His dances sometimes have a strong narrative, such as *Big Bertha* (1971), which depicts a seemingly innocent family whose world is turned upside-down during an outing to an amusement park. He also created such works as *Aureole* (1962), which is a pure movement piece.

Figure 3.9
Paul Taylor in "Aureole," photo by Jack Mitchell. Jerome Robbins Dance Division, The New York Public Library for the Performing Arts, Astor, Lenox and Tilden Foundations.

Throughout the 1950s and 60s, the works of Cunningham, Nikolais and Taylor inspired another group of choreographers to create in a different vein. During the 1960s and 1970s, this new group of post-modern dancers extended the limits, just as Cunningham, Nikolais and Taylor had done, but went even further. Choreographers such as these new post-moderners wanted to reduce dance to its simplest form and to examine what they thought dance really was. Similar to Cunningham and Nikolais, they eliminated the idea of theme and storyline. They also, however, eliminated the use of formal technique, instead examining the basic movements of dance, such as walking, running, skipping and hopping. They began to create dances based on these premises. In order to remain true to these ideas, some of these choreographers refused to work with trained dancers, so many used untrained dancers in their works.

During the 1960s and 1970s, many of these choreographers and dancers performed at the Judson Church in New York (an actual church with a performance space in it), and they came to be known as the Judson Dance Theatre. The dancers were determined to reject the conventional teachings of their predecessors. Dance critic Deborah Jowitt recalled that ". . . it was a reaction against an existing art and also perhaps a comment on the times. Modern dance had become super-charged and the Judson people wanted to express a different kind of rhythm."[3] Visual artists, writers, musicians, as well as dancers came together and presented different types of material that they called dance. They performed in places other than theatres, such as gymnasiums, city streets and even rooftops. They used improvisation, theatre games and other experimental tools in their performances, many of which had the look and feel of the "Happenings" of the 1960s. Happenings were events that were popular with avant garde artists, musicians, writers and dancers and usually involved participation from audiences members. Many of the Judson Dance Theatre members had participated in the Happenings and therefore had experiences in spontaneous and collaborative work and taking risks in dance making.

The beginnings of the Judson Dance Theatre can be traced back to 1960, when Robert Ellis Dunn (1928–1996), began to give composition classes at the Cunningham studio. These classes were experimental in nature and had a strong basis in improvisation and analysis of compositions. In 1962, he organized the first concert at the Judson Church. For a long time, the Judson Dance Theatre was ignored by the press and the dance critics, but had a strong and consistent following. Eventually, it was accepted that "The experiments and adventures of the Judson Dance Theatre . . . laid the groundwork for a post-modern aesthetic in dance that expanded and often challenged the range of purpose, materials, motivations, structures and styles in dance."[4]

After the Judson Dance Theatre disbanded (in 1968), several of its initial members regrouped and, along with new members, formed the Grand Union. The Grand Union was a collaborative effort—there was no specific director and all members had equality. Everyone contributed to the artistic processes of the group. Improvisations containing both dance and theatre were the focus of the company, with some of the material being political, some comical, some abstract and some literal. Sally Banes states that the Grand Union ". . . [stretched] the material and formal limits of their art by incorporating objects (and gestures) from everyday life, using imagery (including sounds) from popular culture and making long, rambling works in a flexible format with a consistently changing stream of images and meanings."[5]

Many important dances were created during the time of the Judson Dance Theatre and the Grand Union. A popular dance from this time was choreographed by Judson Dance Theatre member Yvonne Rainer (b. 1934). This dance, entitled *Trio A* (1966), showed movement that was reduced to its bare essentials. There were no dynamic changes of the movements throughout the dance. Even though some of the movements were fairly difficult to execute, the dancers did not have to be technically trained to perform them. It was acceptable for the audience members to witness dancers struggling with particular movements. Rainer also used this dance as a protest against the Vietnam War. In 1967, she renamed the dance *Convalescent Dance* and performed it on a concert with other protesting choreographers.

It was Rainer, who in 1965 created her *NO Manifesto*, which became the creed of the post-modern movement:

> *No to spectacle no to virtuosity no to transformations and magic and make believe no to glamour and transcendency of the star image no to the heroic no to the anti-heroic no to trash imagery no to involvement of performer or spectator no to style no to camp no to seduction of spectator by the wiles of the performer no to eccentricity no to moving or being moved.*[6]

Trisha Brown (b. 1940), also a Judson Dance Theatre member, gave us *Man Walking Down Side of Building* (1970), which is self-explanatory and was performed in New York City as people on the street looked on. Brown also went on to create many complex choreographic works by using the act of repetition. Simple movement patterns were developed and repeated in several different ways (such as changing the direction, level or timing of the movement), turning the simple, fundamental motor patterns into visually complicated dances. In addition to these choreographers, several others presented dances that had a tremendous impact on the way we now look at dance (see "Major Figures in Modern Dance").

Throughout the 1960s and the 1970s, the post-modern choreographers created works that were a radical departure from the work of their predecessors. During that time, however, some choreographers would not negate technique, theme or storyline and were not considered to be "post-modern." That is to say that their work was not considered to be abstract or avant garde. Alvin Ailey (1931–1990, see Figure 3.10) was one such choreographer and was concerned with making dances that were accessible to the general public. He wanted his audiences to feel totally fulfilled and entertained while they were watching his dances. He was concerned primarily with creating works that had a definite form, unlike the improvised dances of the Judson Dance Theatre and Grand Union. One of Ailey's most popular dances is entitled *Revelations* (1960) and is performed to Negro spirituals. It is a highly technical dance that contains dramatic as well as comical moments. *Revelations*, seen by many as a celebration, depicts the religious heritage of African-Americans. It is still performed today by the Ailey Company and is considered to be their signature dance.

Figure 3.10
Alvin Ailey in "Rite" sequence of *Cinco Latinos.* Jerome Robbins Dance Division, The New York Public Library for the Performing Arts, Astor, Lenox and Tilden Foundations.

DANCE-THEATRE

In the dance world, a great many works fall under the heading of dance-theatre. This genre blends dance and theatre, so that both forms are an integral part of the performance. These performances may include spoken words, text, singing and choreography, which is propelled by theme, dramatics and "theatrics." In the United States, the term *dance-theatre* covers a broad spectrum of creations, but mostly applies to dance companies or choreographers who infuse into their performances dramatic action that is similar to what we see in the theatre. Sometimes, these creations can also come under the heading of "modern dance," because the choreography used is typically from the modern dance genre. For example, some works of the Judson Dance Theatre members, such as Meredith Monk, Lucinda Childs and Yvonne Rainer, can be referred to as dance-theatre, as well as falling under the "post-modern" heading.

Dance-theatre was developed in Europe, specifically in West Germany and came directly out of the modern dance genre:

> *In Europe . . . the development of modern dance was brutally interrupted by World War II. The movement was centered in Germany. Under the Nazis, some modern dance choreographers fled; others collaborated and discredited the movement. By the end of the war, European modern dance was all but wiped out and it did not revive until the sixties, when a new form, the German Tanztheatre, or dance-theatre, rose from the ashes of German expressionist dance of the twenties and thirties.[7]*

It is important to note that in the United States, the *movement*, or the dancing, usually takes priority in dance-theatre work; in Europe, dance-theatre is much more *theatre* than dance. Therefore, there is a great difference between the two continents and what the valued aesthetic is in reference to dance-theatre. Some European dance critics view the American version of dance-theatre as "outdated," while some American critics view the Europeans as negators of dance vocabulary.

One of the major figures in the dance-theatre (or *tanztheatre*) genre in Germany is Pina Bausch (b. 1940), who has been creating works since the late 1960s. Her company, the *Wuppertaler Tanztheatre*, combines dance and theatre to create disturbing pictures of real-life situations. These situations are almost always based on the male/female relationship, which Bausch shows in a bleak and disturbing way. "Especially unresolved are the images of gender and sexual relations. Bausch shows men and women locked into power plays and obsessive patterns of physical and emotional violence."[8] Some American critics do not think that what Bausch creates is dance at all and have called her work "indulgent" and "superficial." On the other hand, other American dance critics feel that Bausch's work is riveting and important and that she presents issues to audiences that must be addressed.

Germany is not the only country where dance-theatre is prominent. France also has a widespread following for dance-theatre, and French choreographers are popular not only in Europe, but in the United States as well. The Japanese dance form Butoh, developed in the 1960s, also falls under the category of dance-theatre. *Butoh* (which is referred to as "dark soul dance" or "dance of utter darkness") is characterized by its use of slow, sustained movements. Sometimes, the performers move at such a slow pace that it is difficult to see them move from one shape to another. One famous company that performs Butoh is Sankai Juku (founded in 1975 by Ushio Amagatsu), whose members have shaved heads and cover their bodies with white makeup for each performance. This company, like many dance-theatre companies, presents painful images of devastation that they perceive to be in the world around them.

MODERN DANCE: TODAY

Today, many choreographers maintain a connection to the traditional modern dance aesthetic, as well as some whose work reflects the philosophy of the post-modern dancers. Still others are forging new ground and carving their own niche in the world of modern dance. It is virtually impossible to categorize or label today's choreographers, because the category of modern dance has become so broad. In today's world of modern dance, there are no rules and regulations, just an underlying freedom to create in whatever way one wishes. To say that in modern dance "anything goes" would be an understatement, since today's choreographers have gone well beyond any traditional definition of what modern dance is.

For example, in recent years aerial, or vertical, dance has become very popular. There are many different companies around the world that call themselves aerial dance companies, but every company has a different aesthetic. There are some companies, for example, that do all of their aerial work outside—on mountain cliffs, in canyons and on rock formations—while other companies utilize indoor spaces and theatres. All of these companies use harnessing and mountain climbing equipment and other special apparatus to perform their dances.

One popular aerial dance company is Project Bandaloop, based in San Francisco. In one event in Houston, the company performed *Romeo and Juliet* on the twenty-third story of a skyscraper. The dancers were 350 feet in the air, while the Houston Symphony played below. It is estimated that there were 40,000 people who viewed that performance. Project Bandaloop also presents outdoor work (on the cliffs of Yosemite, for example), as well as performances in theatres.

Another popular aesthetic that has been seen in the modern dance field is the idea of dance fusion, which is the combining of different dance genres, as well as aspects from theatre, music and visual art. There are many choreographers who blend genres in their work, such as Doug Elkins, Jennifer Muller, and Ron Brown (see "Major Figures in Modern Dance"). In these dances, it is not uncommon to see modern, ballet, jazz, hip hop, African (or another world dance form) all blended together into one dance. There are also choreographers who use text, singing, and other theatrical elements in a dance. These dances not only display a fusion of genres, but sometimes call attention to the multicultural aspects of the art form.

A recent trend in the dance world is the migration of established, professional dancers who are accepting teaching positions in colleges and universities. These mid-career choreographers, such as David Dorfman and Bebe Miller, still maintain a connection to the professional dance world (many still are the artistic directors of a company), but have the security of a full-time position. This situation is a positive one for all parties involved—the universities get to have outstanding artists and educators on their faculty, while the artists have a stable base from which to work.

Of course, there are choreographers who only focus on their company and choreographing for other professional companies. One contemporary choreographer of note is Mark Morris (b. 1956). Morris has created some of today's most critically acclaimed dances and has established himself as an outstanding choreographer. One aspect of Morris's choreography that critics and audiences alike note is his use of music. *Dido and Aeneas* (1989), in which Morris portrayed dual

In today's world of modern dance, there are no rules and regulations, just an underlying freedom to create in whatever way one wishes.

rolls of Dido and the witch, is a clear example of Morris's ability to use music in an extremely sophisticated way. Before Morris choreographs a dance, he studies the musical score and learns every phrase, note and nuance of the piece. Only then will he begin to choreograph. In the end, the audience views a beautiful marriage of dance and music. His dances range from the wildly comic to the dark and dramatic. He is one of today's most famous choreographers, and his company is known world-wide.

Bill T. Jones (b. 1952) is also one of today's most popular modern dance choreographers. He, along with his partner Arnie Zane (1948–1988), created the Bill T. Jones/Arnie Zane Dance Company. Jones's choreography follows a strong narrative and dramatic line. Though it is often controversial (see "Major Figures in Modern Dance"), there is never an absence of passion and feeling in his work. In *D-Man in the Waters* (1989), which Jones created as a tribute to a friend who had died, swimming motifs are combined with subtle gestures in a piece that is at once witty and poignant. In this dance, the dancers explode onto the stage with power, strength and commitment, which are signature qualities of this company.

SUMMARY

All the aforementioned choreographers continued to create dances for many years, and many are still active choreographers today (see "Major Figures in Modern Dance"). Students of modern dance still study the formalized techniques created by many of these artists, while others choose to study with people who teach a more eclectic form. Regardless of the style, technique or method, modern dance has and always will be about the world in which we live, reflecting all that the world encompasses in the form of movement.

The contributions that the post-moderners made to the dance world have had a profound effect on the way that people choreograph and view dance. In providing their audiences with a view of the abstract, they created a rich language of symbolic expression. Writer Selma Jeanne Cohen states:

> *Unquestionably the members of the avant garde have made a significant contribution to the art of dance. They have tremendously broadened the range of the dance vocabulary and revealed its wealth of connotative power. They have explored new relationships between movement and sound, movement and light and color. They have stimulated a fresh awareness of the uniqueness of the medium of dance. If they have not demonstrated that dance must do away with content and narrative or emotional continuity, they have shown that dances can be formed without them.[9]*

Today, the term *post-modern* is used mostly to describe those people active from the 1950s to the 1970s who held to the post-modern aesthetic. A new generation of modern dance choreographers, such as Mark Morris and Bill T. Jones, are referred to in this book as "the next wave" (see "Major Figures in Modern Dance"). Like choreographers past, these new artists provide a contemporary view on issues that range from the mild to the controversial, from the comic to the thought-provoking and from the beautiful to the horrific. The work created by these different artists are based both in reality and in the abstract and provide for the viewers a glimpse into different facets of life.

Dance-theatre is an exciting art form, but one that is defined in different ways, depending on what country you are referring to. In the United States, the movement is usually the primary focus, while in other countries, the theatre aspect takes preference. Although most dance-theatre that is seen worldwide has its roots in modern and post-modern dance, only in the United States is this fact still obvious. Table 3.1 outlines the similarities and differences between traditional modern dance and post-modern dance. Events in modern dance history can be found in Table 3.2.

TABLE 3.1 SIMILARITIES AND DIFFERENCES BETWEEN TRADITIONAL MODERN DANCE AND POST-MODERN DANCE

SIMILARITIES	DIFFERENCES
—both presented dances that displayed innovative movement. —both utilized themes that were social, political and global. —both utilized the elements of space, time and energy in a way that was different from ballet.	—some post-modern dances were plotless and devoid of narrative; many traditional modern dances had strong narrative lines. —traditional modern dances employed trained dancers; some post-modern choreographers used untrained dancers. —traditional modern dances often utilized costumes; post-modern dances were often presented in everyday street clothes. —traditional modern dance was often presented in theatres. Post-modern dance was presented in a number of different places.

TABLE 3.2   OUTLINE OF MODERN DANCE EVENTS

1900	Isadora Duncan has her first solo performances in the United States, which were not well received. She then travels to Europe.
1902	Duncan's first successful performance, which occurs in Budapest.
1903	Duncan travels to Greece to study Greek culture and perform.
1904–1909	Duncan performs several times in Russia; has a major impact on the choreography of Mikhail Fokine.
1914	Ruth St. Denis and Ted Shawn begin Denishawn.
1915	Doris Humphrey becomes a student at Denishawn.
1916	Martha Graham becomes a student at Denishawn.
1920	Charles Weidman becomes a student at Denishawn.
1926	Martha Graham presents her own concert as an independent artist. She then begins to develop her dance company as well as the Graham technique.
1928	Doris Humphrey and Charles Weidman begin the Humphrey-Weidman Dance Company and develop the Humphrey-Weidman technique.
1931	Final Denishawn performance.
1931	The premier of Doris Humphrey's *The Shakers*.
1933	Ted Shawn develops an all-male dance company Ted Shawn and His Male Dancers.
1941	Ted Shawn begins Jacob's Pillow.
1944	Martha Graham choreographs *Appalachian Spring*.
1944	Merce Cunningham creates his first works as an independent artist.
1948	Alwin Nikolais becomes director of the Henry Street Playhouse and develops his own company.
1955	Anna Sokolow creates *Rooms*.
1957	Paul Taylor creates the Paul Taylor Dance Company.
1960	Alvin Ailey choreographs *Revelations*.
1960	Robert Ellis Dunn begins to teach classes at the Judson Church.
1962	The Judson Dance Theatre is formed.
1966	Yvonne Rainer choreographs *Trio A*.
1968	The Grand Union is formed.
1970	Trisha Brown creates *Man Walking Down Side of Building*.
1980	Mark Morris develops the Mark Morris Dance Group.
1982	The Bill T. Jones/Arnie Zane Dance Company is formed.
1988–1991	Mark Morris is the artistic director of the Brussel's *Theatre Royal de la Monnaie*.
1989	Mark Morris choreographs *Dido and Aeneas*.
1989	Bill T. Jones choreographs *D-Man in the Waters*.
1994	Bill T. Jones choreographs *Still/Here*, which dance critic Arlene Croce labels "victim art."
2001	The Mark Morris Dance Center is opened in Brooklyn, N.Y.
2002	Dance Theatre Workshop, a New York City performing institution dedicated to nurturing artistic talent, constructs a new facility. It is called the Bessie in honor of master teacher Bessie Schonberg, and is a state-of-the-art performance space.
2003	Bill T. Jones receives the prestigious Dorothy and Lillian Gish Prize, which recognizes outstanding talents in the arts.
2003	Mark Morris creates a dance, *Non Troppo*, for the leading men of American Ballet Theatre. The work is for a PBS special, *Born to be Wild: The Leading Men of American Ballet Theatre*.
2004	Since the early part of the new century, aerial, or vertical dance has become popular world-wide. Aerial dance has been around since the 1970's but has become a part of mainstream dance in recent years. Some companies performing aerial dance are: Project Bandaloop (San Francisco), Frequent Flyers Productions (Boulder), Stage Fright (London), Legs on the Wall (Australia), and High Strung Aerial Dance (Toronto).

Major Figures in Modern Dance

To give readers a perspective on the wide range of dancers and choreographers who were and are involved in the world of modern dance, here is a list of some of the artists that have helped shape modern dance history.

THE FORERUNNERS

LOIE FULLER (1862–1928, see Figure 6.12)—Fuller was an American dancer who was popular in Europe, particularly in Paris during the late 1800s, where she was known as "La Loie." She developed many lighting techniques and lighting instruments and created visual spectacles by dancing with costumes made from yards of fabrics that would pick up the different colors of the lights. She also encouraged Isadora Duncan to come to Europe, where Duncan was embraced by the public.

ISADORA DUNCAN (1877–1927)—Credited with being the "mother of modern dance," Duncan believed that movements should be drawn from nature. Developing the Duncan technique, comprised of basic movements such as swinging, hopping, running, skipping and leaping, Duncan sought to "free" the body from the confines of ballet and created a truly modern form of dance.

RUTH ST. DENIS (1878–1968)—At first a dancer on the theatrical stage, "Miss Ruth" began to choreograph after seeing a cigarette poster that used the Egyptian goddess Isis in its advertisement. She then became fascinated with Asia and performed for years in Europe and New York. She met and married **Ted Shawn** (1891–1972) and together they formed Denishawn, a school that also had a company that toured throughout the United States. Shawn shared St. Denis's passion for ethnicity, as well as religious expression. In the 1930s their marriage ended, as did the Denishawn school. Shawn established Jacob's Pillow, a school in Massachusetts, and Ted Shawn and His Men Dancers, an all-male dance company that toured throughout the United States for many years. Jacob's Pillow is still in existence today and provides dance instruction and performances in the summers.

RUDOLF VON LABAN (1879–1958)—Sometimes referred to as the "father of German modern dance," Laban is best-known for developing a system of notating dance called Labanotation, as well as a system of notating space, efforts and shapes called Laban Movement Analysis. These two systems are still used today to record and reconstruct dances.

MAUD ALLAN (1883–1956)—Influenced by the work of Isadora Duncan, Allan was a dramatic dancer who also had a great knowledge of music. Like Fuller and Duncan, Allan, an American, became popular in Europe.

MARY WIGMAN (1886–1973)—A German choreographer and dancer whose works are considered to be "expressionistic," Wigman presented dances whose movements were full of meaning and emotion. She is also one of the first modern choreographers to use musical scores consisting mostly of percussion instruments, as well as danced in silence. A student of Laban, she introduced different concepts of spatial designs to her students.

THE PIONEERS

MARTHA GRAHAM (1894–1990)—A Denishawn student, Graham gave her first independent concert in 1926. In 1927, she established the Martha Graham School of Contemporary Dance (still in existence today) and a company comprised of all women. She later expanded her company to include male dancers. Graham's dances, most of them psychological dramas, were primarily based on themes drawn from Greek mythology, American pioneers and American Indians. Graham developed a dance technique based on a system of contraction and release of the center of the body.

DORIS HUMPHREY (1895–1958)—A Denishawn student, Humphrey eventually became a teacher at the school and developed, along with Ruth St. Denis, a technique known as "music visualization," in which movement phrases, patterns and rhythms correspond with musical phrases, patterns and rhythms (and enables one to "visualize" the music). In 1928, she left Denishawn and together with **CHARLES WEIDMAN** (1901–1975), another Denishawn student, developed the Humphrey-Weidman School and Dance Company. They developed a dance technique that revolved around fall and recovery, with a major emphasis on balance. Their company disbanded in 1945 and Humphrey became artistic director of the José Limon Dance Company (Limon was one of her students). Weidman went out on his own and choreographed dances, many of a comic nature. Weidman was truly gifted in the act of pantomime and had a wonderful sense of comic timing.

HANYA HOLM (1898–1992)—A student of Mary Wigman, Holm came to the United States in 1931 to establish a Wigman school. For a short time she had a company and became a master teacher using the theories of Wigman as well as her own. Holm is also known as one of the first modern dance choreographers to choreograph for musicals on Broadway such as *Kiss Me Kate, Out of This World* and *My Fair Lady.*

KURT JOOSS (1901–1979)—Jooss was also a student of Laban and he carried much of Laban's principles into his own work. He is famous for choreographing *The Green Table,* in 1932, which was a protest against war.

THE SECOND GENERATION

MARTHA HILL (1900–1995)—One of the best-known dance educators, Hill established the first bachelor of arts degree in dance at Bennington College in 1932. She is also credited with providing teaching and performing opportunities for Martha Graham, Doris Humphrey, Charles Weidman and Hanya Holm, first at Bennington College, and then at the newly established American Dance Festival. In 1951, she created the dance division of the Julliard School, where dancers from all over the world still train.

HELEN TAMIRIS (1905–1966)—Tamiris came to modern dance through the ballet world. In 1927, she began to choreograph solo dances for herself. She also choreographed several musical theatre productions such as *Show Boat* and *Annie Get Your Gun.* She is best-known for creating a dance called *Negro Spirituals.* Although she was white, she was the first choreographer to use these spirituals for concert dance. She often collaborated with **Daniel Nagrin** (b. 1917), who is known for his choreography and master teaching, particularly in the areas of improvisation and composition.

LESTER HORTON (1906–1953)—A West Coast choreographer, Horton developed his company in 1932 and was focused on presenting works depicting American Indian culture. He developed the Horton technique, which requires a strong torso and symmetrical and asymmetrical movements of the arms and legs.

JOSÉ LIMON (1908–1972)—A student of Humphrey and Weidman, Limon was a Mexican-American whose heritage influenced his work. After World War II, he formed the José Limon Dance Company and, using the principles of weight, and fall and recovery, developed a technique that was closely linked to the technique of Humphrey and Weidman.

KATHERINE DUNHAM (b. 1912)—In 1931, Dunham had her first concert in Chicago entitled *Negro Rhapsody.* This concert was to be the beginnings of black concert dance. Dunham is known for combining native Caribbean and modern dance and is also known as a researcher and a scholar. She appeared in several musical theatre productions as well as movie musicals, and her work also had an influence on jazz dance.

BONNIE BIRD (1914–1995)—Bird's career includes both academic and professional performing experiences. She was one of the first dancers in Martha Graham's dance company and also served as her teaching assistant. She was a prolific writer and wrote for many of today's leading dance periodicals and magazines. She also served as the Head of International Development at the Laban Centre of Movement and Dance in London.

ANNA SOKOLOW (1915–2000)—One of the first members of the Martha Graham Company, Sokolow also worked during that time as an independent choreographer. Over the years, Sokolow developed professional and personal relationships with dancers in Mexico and Israel and traveled to these places to teach and choreograph. Sokolow's dances were both political and social comments on societal issues.

BELLA LEWITZKY (1916–2004)—Lewitzky was a student of Lester Horton. Her choreography is most noted for its intricate movement patterns and strong technique. She is recognized as a champion for freedom of expression and anti-censorship. The Lewitzky Dance Company was housed for many years in Los Angeles, but has since disbanded.

ERICK HAWKINS (1917–1994)—Hawkins was originally a ballet dancer and became the first male dancer to join Martha Graham's dance company. He later became her husband. After their breakup, he left her company and in 1951 began to establish himself as an independent choreographer. He created a new technique that put emphasis on ease and free flow of movements. Today, the Hawkins School in New York and the Erick Hawkins Dance Company are still a viable part of the dance community.

VALERIE BETTIS (1919–1982)—Bettis, a student of Hanya Holm, was known as a master teacher as well as a choreographer. She is also credited with being one of the first modern dancers to choreograph on a ballet company (the Ballet Russes de Monte Carlo).

PEARL PRIMUS (1919–1994)—A student of Graham, Humphrey, Weidman and Holm, Primus is also credited with bringing black concert dance to the forefront. In her choreography, her focus was mainly on African dance and African subject matter. In contrast to Dunham, whose movements were flowing and smooth, Primus' movements were athletic and dynamic (see Figure 6.13).

TALLEY BEATTY (c. 1923–1996)—Beatty performed in the first company that Katherine Dunham established. He eventually established his own company, which performed for about five years. His choreography combined modern and jazz techniques and often revealed the racial injustice suffered by African-Americans. One of his most popular dances is *The Road of the Phoebe Snow,* created in 1959, which portrayed life along the famous railroad line.

DONALD MCKAYLE (b. 1930)—McKayle studied with Graham and Cunningham, among others. His choreography calls attention to the black experience and is currently performed by such companies as the Dayton Contemporary Dance Company and the Alvin Ailey American Dance Theatre.

ALVIN AILEY (1931–1990)—A student of Lester Horton, Ailey developed his own company in the mid-1950s. Called the Alvin Ailey American Dance Theatre, the company is located in New York. Ailey was always concerned with making his dances accessible to the audience. He combined modern, jazz and world dance to create a unique style. The Ailey company, still in existence today, is world-renowned.

ELEO POMARE (b. 1937)—Like Beatty's works, Pomare's choreography often represents the struggles of blacks in America. His powerful *Blues for the Jungle*, created in 1972, is a realistic look at life in Harlem. He studied with Kurt Jooss in Germany and eventually established his own company that made their New York City debut in 1966.

THE POST-MODERNERS

ALWIN NIKOLAIS (1912–1993)—A student of Hanya Holm, "Nik" is best remembered for his choreography that explores the use of lighting, costumes and props in a purely theatrical way. Nik was not concerned with showing emotion on stage, but rather motion, and is known as one of the forerunners of the post-modern movement. In 1970, along with fellow choreographer **Murray Louis** (b. 1926), he established the Nikolais-Louis Dance Lab in New York, as well as the Nikolais-Louis Dance Company established in later years. Louis, once a student of Nikolais, continues the artistic directorship of the Nikolais-Louis Dance Company.

MERCE CUNNINGHAM (b. 1919)—Cunningham came to dance because of tap dance lessons he received at a young age. He was a dancer with the Martha Graham Dance Company for five years before establishing the Merce Cunningham Dance Company in 1953. He developed the Cunningham technique, in which the spine acts as a spring and can coil, twist and turn. His technique also employs intricate direction changes and many shifts of weight throughout a given phrase of movement. He created dances that were devoid of meaning and were "movement for movement's sake." He is credited with being "the father of post-modern dance."

ANNA HALPRIN (b. 1920)—One of the leading figures in the Judson Dance Theatre, Halprin had, as a student, studied the more formalized techniques of her predecessors. Today, she is best-known for her work in improvisation.

PAUL TAYLOR (b. 1930)—In a career spanning both the modern and post-modern movements, Taylor was both a student of Martha Graham and a dancer with the Merce Cunningham Dance Company. He is considered to be one of the forerunners of the post-modern movement. In 1955, Taylor began to create his own dances and in 1961 formed his own company. Taylor's choreography is a combination of athletic dynamics and beauty. Today, the Paul Taylor Dance Company is world-renowned.

THE POST-MODERNERS: SECOND GENERATION

ROBERT ELLIS DUNN (1929–1996)—Dunn, a musician, gave dance composition and improvisation classes at the Cunningham School in the 1960s. In 1962, he organized the first dance concert at the Judson Memorial Church in New York and thus began the activities of the Judson Dance Theatre.

VIOLA FARBER (1931–1998)—As a choreographer, Farber was very much influenced by her former teacher, Merce Cunningham, although some of her works were on the comical side. Farber began her own company in 1953. She is also known for succeeding Alwin Nikolais as artistic director of the *Centre National de Dance Contemporaine* in France.

DAN WAGONER (b. 1932)—Wagoner came to New York in the late 1950s and danced with the Martha Graham, Merce Cunningham and Paul Taylor companies before he established his own company in 1969. Dan Wagoner and Dancers performed for almost twenty-five years, but had to disband because of financial reasons.

YVONNE RAINER (b. 1934)—A student of Cunningham, Rainer was one of the founding members of the Judson Dance Theatre. Rainer was concerned with reducing dance to a minimum, without emotion, theatricality or spectacle. Today, Rainer is still an active choreographer.

SIMONE FORTI (b. 1935)—A student of Anna Halprin, Forti's works took on an improvisational feel, much like those of her teacher. Today, a master teacher herself, Forti continues to create works from an improvisational base.

ROD RODGERS (1938–2002)—For several years, Rodgers was a member of the Erick Hawkins Dance Company. In the mid-1960s he formed the Rod Rodgers Dance Company, which performed choreography that was a mix of modern and jazz. He was also a founding member of the Association of Black Choreographers.

STEVE PAXTON (b. 1939)—Paxton is best-known for developing "contact improvisation" (see Chapter Seven: Improvisation and Creative Movement). Paxton was also a founding member of the Judson Dance Theatre and was a student of Cunningham.

TRISHA BROWN (b. 1940, see Figure 6.14)—Another founding member of the Judson Dance Theatre, Brown's choreography employed the use of repetition. She created intricate movement patterns that seemed to logically build from one movement to the next. Today, the Trisha Brown Dance Company performs worldwide.

LUCINDA CHILDS (b. 1940)—Another student of Cunningham and founding member of the Judson Dance Theatre, Child's use of repetition of movement and phrases were a trademark of her choreography. In recent years, Childs has provided choreography for mixed-media performances such as Robert Wilson's *Einstein on the Beach*.

GUS SOLOMONS, JR. (b. 1940)—Solomons danced with the Martha Graham and Cunningham Dance Companies, among others. In addition to choreographing, Solomons is a dance reviewer for *Dance Magazine* and other publications.

TWYLA THARP (b. 1942)—Tharp worked with both Cunningham and Taylor and later developed her own company and created a movement style that was a blend of several dance forms, including ballet, modern, tap and jazz. Although seemingly "loose," Tharp's choreography is technically difficult, with its use of a relaxed torso but dynamically charged arm and leg movements. Tharp has also choreographed on several ballet companies and for a short while was a resident choreographer for American Ballet Theatre in New York. In 2002, she created the Broadway musical *Movin' Out*, with music by Billy Joel.

DAVID GORDON (b. 1943)—Once a student of Cunningham and founding member of the Judson Dance Theatre (as well as its offspring, the Grand Union), Gordon has been choreographing since the early 1960s. His dances, many filled with comical moments, combined movement and text. The David Gordon Pick-Up Company is comprised of dancers who are also skilled actors, including Gordon's wife, Valda Setterfield (b. 1934).

MEREDITH MONK (b. 1943)—Another student of Cunningham, Monk combined her talents as a musician and writer within her works. Her dance aesthetic differed from most of the Judson Dance Theatre members in that her dances were full of symbolism and emotion. Today, Monk presents mixed-media events that include her original choreography, music and text.

LAR LUBOVITCH (b. 1944)—A student of Martha Graham, Anna Sokolow and José Limon, Lubovitch danced with a number of modern dance companies before creating his own. His choreography, which combines highly charged movement phrases with intricate floor patterns, has made his company one of the best-loved in America.

MARGARET JENKINS (b. 1944)—Jenkins is the artistic director of the Margaret Jenkins Dance Company, which has been based in San Francisco for over twenty years. She creates narrative works in which the dancers, through the use of improvisation and the development of movement phrases, are often collaborators.

LAURA DEAN (b. 1945)—The use of repetition, particularly spinning and spins that move in intricate patterns around the stage, are among the tools that Dean used in her choreography. She was a Cunningham student and a founding member of the Judson Dance Theatre. Today, her company, Laura Dean Musicians and Dancers, still employs the techniques she developed in the 1960s.

ULYSSES DOVE (1947–1996)—Dove performed with many leading dance companies, such as the Merce Cunningham Dance Company and the Alvin Ailey American Dance Theatre. His choreography received critical acclaim, and has been seen on such companies as the American Ballet Theatre, New York City Ballet and Alvin Ailey American Dance Theatre.

KEI TAKEI—A choreographer whose dances appear to be as sacred as primitive rituals, Takei came to the United States from Japan in 1966. Her use of repetition is essential in her work, which has a mesmerizing effect on the audience. Her company, Moving Earth Orient Sphere, has been performing a series of dances for many years, all with the word "light" in the title.

THE NEXT WAVE

PINA BAUSCH (b. 1940)—Bausch is a German choreographer whose company *Wuppertaler Tanztheatre* (dance-theatre), combines dance and theatre to create disturbing pictures of real-life situations. Many of her dances deal with gender issues, specifically focusing on fear and brutality.

GARTH FAGAN (b. 1940)—Jamaican-born Fagan was a student of Martha Graham, Pearl Primus and Alvin Ailey, among others. His company, Garth Fagan Dance, uniquely blends modern, jazz and world dance. Based in Rochester, New York, his company is internationally known. He also created the choreography for the Broadway production of *The Lion King*.

JUDITH JAMISON (b. 1944)—Jamison was one of Alvin Ailey's principal dancers for many years. He created several roles and dances specifically for her, including the beautiful solo *Cry*. After Ailey's death in 1990, Jamison assumed the position of artistic director of the Alvin Ailey American Dance Theatre.

LIZ LERMAN (b. 1947)—One of our country's most political choreographers, Lerman's dances are always a commentary on societal and political issues. The use of dance and text is a trademark of her work, as is her intergenerational dance company, The Dance Exchange. Lerman also directs Dancers of the Third Age, a company with members over age sixty.

BEBE MILLER (b. 1949)—Miller's works are among today's most highly acclaimed in the modern dance world. Using a variety of music, such as classical pieces and the music of Jimi Hendrix, Miller's works are thought-provoking and dramatic.

ELIZABETH STREB (b. 1950)—Streb's company, Elizabeth Streb/Ringside, is known for its fierce athleticism that has sometimes been called "violent," although she does not see it as such. Streb has expanded the definition of dance to include movements that seem to defy gravity and use space unlike any other dance company. Her dances often include props or set pieces, such as walls or boxes, that the movements center around, in, under, over, etc., and provide the viewer with images unlike any they have ever seen before in a dance concert.

MAGUY MARIN (b. 1951)—A Spaniard born and raised in France, Marin trained in classical ballet as a young child and was eventually introduced to modern dance. She danced in Maurice Béjart's company for three years, and then eventually established the *Compagnie Maguy Marin*. Her choreography has been categorized as dance-theatre, and she is known as one of France's most innovative choreographers. Some of her most popular works, such as *Cinderella* and *Coppelia*, were created for the Lyons Opera Ballet.

EIKO (b. 1951) **and Koma** (b. 1947)—These dancers from Japan present what seems to be Butoh-inspired choreography, although they refer to their technique as "Delicious Movement." Their movements are performed so slowly that at times the audience does not see their transition from one movement to the next. Their dances usually have dark and dramatic themes.

JOE GOODE (b. 1951)—Goode resides on the West Coast where he is a choreographer, theatre director and teacher. After dancing with the Margaret Jenkins Dance Company, he formed the Joe Goode Performance Group (in 1985). Mostly all of his dances incorporate movement, music, text and singing. Much of the work he creates has been influenced by the HIV/AIDS epidemic.

RALPH LEMON (b. 1952)—Lemon's emotion-filled dances were the driving force of his popular company (which has disbanded). He is concerned with showing real ideas and real people in his works. His unique movement style combines physical strength and strong technique with pedestrian gestures and free-flowing movements.

OHAD NAHARIN (b. 1952)—Naharin began dancing with the Batsheva Dance Company in Israel. He was then invited by Martha Graham to join her company in New York. While there, he was also a scholarship student at the School of American Ballet. In 1980, he made his debut as a choreographer, and to date has choreographed on major dance companies, including Nederlands Dans Theatre, Frankfurt Ballet, Hubbard Street Dance and Rambert Dance Company.

BILL T. JONES (b. 1952, see Figure 6.15)—Artistic director of the Bill T. Jones/Arnie Zane Dance Company (*Zane is now deceased, a victim of the AIDS virus*), Jones's choreography follows a strong narrative and dramatic line. Including dances that involve nudity, Jones's dances are both poignant and controversial. One of his dances, *Still/Here* (1994), created a major controversy. Because of Jones's use of people with terminal illnesses in the dance, critic Arlene Croce refused to review the dance, which she said was "victim art." Because of this disagreement, the dance world, as well as the popular media, began a long and heated debate on "victim art" and Jones's *Still/Here*.

PEGGY BAKER (b. 1953)—Baker, a Canadian, has won international acclaim for her choreography and performances. From 1981–88, she was a dancer and rehearsal director with the Lar Lubovitch Dance Company. In 1990, she toured with Mikhail Baryshnikov's White Oak Dance Project. Today, she is the Artistic Director of Peggy Baker/Solo Dance.

MARGIE GILLIS (b. 1953)—Gillis is a Canadian artist mostly known for her solo work. Her ability as a solo artist is outstanding and she is known world-wide as a spectacular performer. She has said that she uses dance as a catharsis to express joy, sorrow and uncertainty.

MOLISSA FENLEY (b. 1954)—Once the artistic director of a small company, Fenley, since 1987, has been performing almost exclusively as a solo artist. Her works are primarily abstract and her movements are a display of pure, clean lines.

HOMER AVILA (1955–2004)—A dancer with Momix and the Bill T. Jones/Arnie Zane Dance Company, Avila was an outstanding performer. In 2001, he lost a leg and hip to a rare form of cancer, but continued to perform even after his surgery. A dedicated and inspiring performer, Avila performed up until the time he died.

MARK MORRIS (b. 1956)—One of today's leading choreographers, Morris is well-known for his sophisticated use of music in his dances. Now residing in the United States, his company also had a three-year residency in Brussels, where he was the artistic director of the *Theatre Royal de la Monnaie*. In 2001, the Mark Morris Dance Center was opened in Brooklyn, NY.

DAVID DORFMAN (b. 1956)—Dorfman came to dance late in life, having been an athlete throughout much of his youth. He began dancing in college, and though he had originally set out to be in the business world, he ended up receiving an M.F.A. degree in dance. He now has a company, David Dorfman Dance, which is based in New York and performs dynamically and emotionally charged dances, often blending movement, music and text. He has also been known to do community projects, working with people of all levels of dance experience.

SUSAN MARSHALL (b. 1958)—Marshall formed her dance company, Susan Marshall and Company, in 1982. She is known for taking gestures and pedestrian movements and utilizing them in her highly dynamic and athletic choreography. She is concerned with showing emotion and human interaction in her choreography.

STEPHEN PETRONIO (b. 1958)—Petronio danced with Trisha Brown from 1979–1986. In 1984, he founded the Stephen Petronio Dance Company. Petronio has been known to create very emotional and intellectual dances, and often uses costumes that blur and confuse sexual identity.

DAVID PARSONS (b. 1959)—Parsons was a dancer with the Paul Taylor Dance Company for nine years. He left Taylor's company in 1987 to begin his own, the Parsons Dance Company, which is internationally known today. Parsons' choreography is dynamically charged and he encompasses a broad range of emotions in his dance repertory.

JENNIFER MULLER (b. 195?)—Jennifer Muller/The Works is a company that often blends several genres into one dance. It is not uncommon to see a Muller work that includes modern, ballet, jazz, text and singing. Her work is sometimes referred to as dance theatre. Another signature of her choreography is the inventive partnering sequences that her dancers perform.

DOUG VARONE (b. 195?)—Varone's company, Doug Varone and Dancers, is one of the most dynamic and exciting companies performing today. Varone is extremely versatile, creating dances that range from being abstract to those that have strong emotional content. In 1997, he choreographed and staged a Broadway musical, *Triumph of Love*.

DOUG ELKINS (b. 1960)—A self-proclaimed "style thief," Elkins combines ballet and modern dance with break dancing and hip-hop to create his unusual choreography. In his dances, Elkins presents the audience with humorous contradictions, such as men in women's clothing and break dancing done in Catholic school uniforms.

SEAN CURRAN (b. 1961)—Formerly a dancer with Bill T. Jones/Arnie Zane Dance Company, Curran is now an exceptional choreographer in his own right. After performing in the Broadway show *Stomp* for four years, Curran began making and presenting dances that are personal expressions shown through a wide range of themes and dynamics.

MICHAEL CLARK (b. 1962)—Formerly a ballet dancer, Clark came to modern dance after arriving in the United States from Britain and studying at the Cunningham school. He is one of Britain's most controversial choreographers. His dances, many of which use rock music and stylized clothing, are some of the most innovative dances seen today.

JOHN JASPERSE (b. 1963)—Jasperse began to choreograph and perform professionally in 1985. In 1989, he established the John Jasperse Company. He is known for doing experimental work influenced by a post modern aesthetic.

ANDREA WOODS (b. 1964)—Woods is the Artistic Director of Souloworks/Andrea E. Woods and Dancers based in Brooklyn, NY. She performed with Bill T. Jones/Arnie Zane Dance Company from 1989–95. She is a dynamic performer with powerful stage presence. Her work is created with inspiration from the African American experience and presented as African American folklore.

RON BROWN (b. 1966)—Brown is the founder and artistic director of the Ronald K. Brown/Evidence Dance Company. In his choreography, he fuses modern dance with West African dance, a combination that is exciting and inspiring to observe. His highly physical choreography has been described as storytelling through the body. Today, he is one of the most sought-after choreographers, setting dances on college students as well as professional dancers, such as those of the Alvin Ailey American Dance Theatre.

CHAPTER 4

Jazz Dance, Musical Theatre and Tap Dance

INTRODUCTION

The world of jazz dance, musical theatre and tap dance is an exciting and thrilling one. This chapter explores these American dance forms that all have their roots in African movements and rhythms.

JAZZ DANCE

Jazz dance is an exciting dance genre that today has a place in the popular theatre and the concert stage, in small dance studios and large universities and in movies and television. The history of jazz dance is a fascinating one, beginning with the origins that can be traced back to Africa.

In the seventeenth century, when slaves were brought to America from Africa, they brought with them their music and dance. The dancing and drumming that was so much a part of African life was continued by the slaves on the plantations. Eventually, the slave masters prohibited drumming, but the African rhythms did not diminish. They were kept alive by the slaves who clapped their hands, stomped their feet and sang the songs of their motherland.[1] On the plantations, dances were performed for enjoyment and also for entertainment and competitions. Slave masters would often have the best dancers entertain their guests or compete against slaves from other plantations.

Eventually, the songs and dances of these people were brought into the theatres, but not by the people who had created them. The Minstrel shows, beginning in the 1830s, showcased black songs and dances. But since blacks were not allowed to perform on a public stage (with the exception of those such as "Master Juba"—see "Major Figures in Jazz Dance, Musical Theatre and Tap Dance"), whites in blackface appeared before the audiences, performing parodies of the songs and dances of the black culture. It wasn't until the 1860s that blacks began to appear in their own Minstrel shows,[2] where they performed for other blacks as well as Irish immigrants. Eventually, the black minstrel shows became as popular as the white minstrels, in part because of a section of the shows (usually the close of the first act) called the "cakewalk." The cakewalk, which came directly from

The history of jazz dance is a fascinating one, beginning with the origins that can be traced back to Africa.

69

plantation entertainments, ". . . was a contest among dancing couples who attempted to outdo each other in the mock imitation of the white man's manners and behavior."[3] During the cakewalk, the dancers displayed their best struts, high kicks and show-stopping footwork.

The minstrels remained popular until the early 1900s and paved the way for the vaudeville, revue and burlesque shows that were to dominate the American stage for the next twenty years. Although all three theatrical entertainments were popular, none was as popular or as significant to jazz dance history as the vaudeville show. Writer Richard Kislan provides an explanation of the importance of the Vaudeville era:

> More than any other entertainment alternative in its time, Vaudeville encouraged, if not precipitated, the quantitative and varietal expansion of dance acts before the public. Most vaudeville circuits included at least one song-and-dance act or minimusical revue on the bill. The system valued uniqueness and encouraged diversity. Some dancers traded on talent or technique; others developed unusual material. There were Dutch dancers, Russian dancers, Irish dancers, blackface minstrel dancers, whiteface minstrel dancers, flash acts, class acts, toe dancers, knockabouts, acrobatic dancers, competition acts and legomania. Even the celebrated originators of modern dance—Martha Graham, Doris Humphrey and Charles Weidman—did their stints in vaudeville. . . . It served as a professional school, a training ground and an experimental station for the dancers destined for Broadway, nightclubs and film. . . .[4]

Today, the use of syncopated rhythms is what, for many, characterizes jazz dance.

The Vaudeville era showcased a wealth of song and dance performers. It is important to remember the contributions that African-American performers gave to this era. Though the lives of these performers were difficult, black dancers continued to create and perform new movements, keeping the African connection to the earth (hence the repeated use of the plie in jazz dance) and to the African rhythms. The Vaudeville era also marked the emergence of jazz music (around 1919), which was a combination of ragtime and the blues.[5] Eventually, dancers began to connect to the syncopated rhythms of jazz music. Today, the use of syncopated rhythms is what, for many, characterizes jazz dance.[6]

The advent of Latin jazz music also had an influence on the dance form. In the 19th century, a fusion of African rhythms and traditional music from the Caribbean and the United States came to be known as Latin Jazz. Evident in this music is the use of the *clave*, an instrument comprised of two wooden sticks that are hit together to produce a high pitched sound. *Clave* also refers to the specific rhythmic pattern found in Latin jazz, and that dances such as the Salsa utilize. In Latin jazz, it is not uncommon for the body to have ". . . several axes of motion. [The body] can move forward and back, up and down, and the hips create possibilities for lateral movement. Latin American dance . . . is grounded in African rhythms, which are polyrhythmic . . . there are several layers of rhythm going on at the same time."[7]

The Harlem Renaissance (1921–1933) was another significant time period in the history of jazz dance. Harlem, New York, was the place for all high-society people to see and be seen. At this time, many exclusive clubs opened, probably the most famous being the Cotton Club. These clubs, which catered to a white clientele, had elaborate floor shows where black singers and dancers performed. Because of the popularity of these clubs and their shows, employment for black dancers was plentiful during the Harlem Renaissance. This decade, known as the Roaring Twenties, saw many dances that were performed at these clubs, such as the Charleston and the Black Bottom, become part of a dance craze. The Charleston became immensely popular in the United States and eventually in Europe—everyone wanted to learn how to dance the Charleston. "Flappers," or women who wore their hair in a short bob and wore short, fringed dresses, are usually equated with the Charleston. There are movements in the Charleston, however, that can be traced back to African dances and also to dances in certain parts of Haiti.

During the next few decades, jazz dance was a part of the theatre, nightclubs, movie musicals, dance concerts and dance studios. During the 1950s and the 1960s, television provided the public with many images of jazz dance, mostly through variety shows such as "The Lawrence Welk Show" and "The Ed Sullivan Show." Although much of the "television dance" that was seen at that time would probably appear very dated to a contemporary audience, many great artists regularly danced on television—Fred Astaire, Gene Kelly, Ann Miller and Ray Bolger, to name a few. There were also outstanding musical theatre productions created during this time for both stage and screen (see "Musical Theatre").

Today, jazz dance encompasses several different styles of movement and has come to represent a number of different things to different people. While "jazz dance" has been defined in several ways, descriptive terms such as *sensual, visceral, improvisational, syncopated, hot* and *cool* are often used in reference to jazz dance. Dancers/writers Mike Moore and Liz Williamson provide an excellent description of jazz dance by stating:

> Basically, jazz is an approach. It is everchanging, but vitality is a constant. A continual refinement is also constant. Changes in jazz happen in very subtle ways. Jazz dancers seek the fine edge of perfection in their performance. No movement is dull, there is an unabated theatricality about jazz. No movement is perfunctory. Improvisation is the core. Jazz dance moves through delicate changes of color and shading. In jazz dance, one works toward an individual style that builds from traditional jazz origins and strikes out boldly in the contemporary. Jazz was born in America, of African parents.[8]

As stated earlier, the term *jazz dance* has come to mean a lot of different things to different people. Certain characteristics of jazz dance, however, are essential and cannot be ignored. Today, so much of what is called jazz dance is concerned only with superficial movements. Many recent choreographers (particularly those who work in a commercial vein) appear to believe that performing certain "dance tricks," such as high kicks and multiple turns, will please and win over audiences. This idea might be true to a certain extent, but choreographers and audiences alike must realize that there is more to a dance than staying in one place and dancing at one set speed and rhythm, which seems to be prevalent in some jazz dance choreography. Changing levels, directions, shapes and floor patterns are an essential part of *all* choreography and should also be included in jazz dance choreography. In addition, focal changes and movements incorporating space should be considered. Also, the use of diagonal, curved or asymmetrical lines might be more interesting than presenting a group of dancers who face the audience in a symmetrical formation for an entire dance.

The use of music and movement in relation to phrasing is an important aspect of jazz dance. Today, some jazz dances are very "square," with all of the movements happening on the "one" count. Although this use of rhythm might be appropriate for part of a dance, the use of the syncopated rhythm is a specific characteristic of jazz dance and should be used in jazz choreography. The use of varying rhythms and dynamics will enhance a jazz dance tremendously. There is much more appeal in viewing jazz choreography that brings the audience through a range of energy than in watching a dance that stays at the same energy level throughout.

Of course, style is also an important aspect of jazz dance. Richard Kislan describes style as ". . . the specific manner of expression peculiar to a work, a period, or a personality. It implies the purposeful and consistent choice of expressive ingredients to achieve a characteristic manner"[9] Can style be taught? Maybe. Should it be encouraged? Definitely. Dancers should be encouraged to develop their own personal style. This personal style is developed when a dancer totally commits every aspect of himself or herself to the movement, including energy, focus, facial expression and intent, while remaining true to the character or situation that the choreographer has created. Additionally, many different categories fall under the rubric of jazz dance styles—musical theatre dance, tap, lyrical, funk, swing and Latin jazz (to name a few)—which dancers and choreographers can study and work in.

The use of music and movement in relation to phrasing is an important aspect of jazz dance.

MUSICAL THEATRE

Early examples of musical theatre productions can be found in eighteenth-century England, France and Germany, although some historians argue that the musical performances the Ancient Greeks and Romans produced were the actual predecessors to what we today call musical theatre. Whenever the beginnings of musical theatre, the advent of the American musical theatre production is an integral part of the history of dance (as well as theatre). American musical theatre dance has its roots in jazz dance. One of the first musical theatre productions of note was *The Black Crook*. In 1866, *The Black Crook* was directed by David Costa and was the first theatre piece to use dance to move the storyline along. This work is significant because after this production, dance was seen as a positive and useful "tool," and thus was included in many theatrical productions.

There were many significant happenings in the history of musical theatre dance. One such happening was the creation of the first "Negro" musical in 1921, called *Shuffle Along*, created by a team of talented writers, actors and song-makers, including jazz great Eubie Blake (1883–1983). *Shuffle Along* paved the way for the African-American performer:

> *[It] was the first outstanding Negro musical to play white theatres from coast to coast . . . and Negro musicals flourished on Broadway for a decade or so. Attentions were focused on the talents of the Negro in vernacular comedy, song and dance and jobs opened up for Negro performers. Above all, musical comedy took on a new and rhythmic life and chorus girls began learning to dance jazz.[10]*

One such chorus girl was a protégée of Eubie Blake's named Josephine Baker (1906–1975), who became a popular international star. She also popularized several dances of the 1920s, including the Charleston and the Black Bottom.

Another significant happening in the history of musical theatre dance was in 1926, when dance director Seymour Felix (1892–1961) introduced the marriage of book (script), music, lyrics and dance as an important aspect of musical theatre. While working on the Rodgers and Hart musical *Peggy Ann*, Felix was determined to

> . . . *devise "atmospheric" numbers, dances that unfold gradually and consist of development and climax as if they were dramatic units themselves instead of "a mere pounding of feet and kicking to music." Colorful dances could be and spectacle they could embrace, but harmonize with the story they must—and did. Then as now, the secret to successful integration of show dances lay in the discovery of valid motives for the movement. . . . Once he recognized the dependence of the dance ensemble on book, music and lyrics, Felix sought to ensure a more unified effect onstage by coordinating his efforts with that of the show's creators.[11]*

From that time on, theatre productions highlighting dance sequences were the norm and were also enthusiastically received by the audiences. In 1943, Agnes de Mille (1905–1993), another pioneer of musical theatre choreography, choreographed *Oklahoma* and presented dance in a way that had never been presented before. Until this time, dances in musicals were inserted to move the storyline, or for sheer entertainment purposes. De Mille's choreography superseded this, creating on the stage and screen a truly artistic representation of dance. In *Oklahoma*, one of the most popular dance sections is commonly known as the "dream sequence." Here, the dancers perform a surrealistic dance number whose duration is almost fifteen minutes. While adding to the storyline, this sequence is also a dramatic work unto itself, depicting frantic emotion in a nightmarish setting. The validity and artistry of de Mille's work gave musical theatre choreographers the respect they deserved, putting them on equal status with the director, composer and playwright.

The validity and artistry of de Mille's work gave musical theatre choreographers the respect they deserved, putting them on equal status with the director, composer and playwright.

Many choreographers, who were primarily known as ballet or modern dance choreographers, created outstanding dances and dance sequences for musical theatre productions. For example, ballet greats George Balanchine, Agnes de Mille and Jerome Robbins all choreographed for musical theatre productions. Modern dance choreographers such as Katherine Dunham, Helen Tamiris, Hanya Holm, Valerie Bettis and Twyla Tharp also produced musical theatre works. There were, however, a number of people who were considered choreographers and dance directors who worked exclusively in the jazz dance and musical theatre genres. One such choreographer was Jack Cole (1913–1974).

It is interesting to note that Cole began his career in dance by studying with modern dance greats such as Ruth St. Denis and Ted Shawn and Doris Humphrey and Charles Weidman. He was very much influenced by the teachings of the Denishawn school, particularly the emphasis on Eastern dance styles. Therefore, he ". . . developed an entirely personal mode of jazz-ethnic-ballet that prevails as the dominant look of and technique for dancing in today's musicals, films, nightclub revues, television commercials and videos."[12] Many other choreographers who worked in the jazz dance and musical theatre idiom, such as Jerome Robbins, Bob Fosse and Gower Champion, were greatly influenced by Cole's style.

One of Cole's most popular productions was *Kismet* (1955), where his Eastern dance influence is clearly seen in the choreography depicting the story of the Arabian Nights. Many consider Cole to be the "father of jazz dance," and the style that he developed in the 1940s is still prevalent in today's jazz dance choreography.

The realm of musical theatre belongs to both the theatrical stage and the movie musical. Many musical theatre productions are seen first as live theatre and are then recreated for the movie screen. The making of a Broadway musical is quite an undertaking, mostly because of the astronomical expense required for such productions. Some popular musical theatre productions were/are *West Side Story* (1961), *The King and I* (1951), *Chicago* (1975, and revived in 1996), *A Chorus Line* (1974), *Cats* (1981), *Kiss of the Spider Woman* (1992), *Tommy* (1993), *Beauty and the Beast* (1994), *Rent* (1996), *The Lion King* (1997), *Aida* (2000), *The Producers* (2001), *Mama Mia* (2001), *Hairspray* (2002), *Movin' Out* (2002), *Wicked* (2003), *Bombay Dreams* (2004) and *Brooklyn* (2004).

TAP DANCE

Tap dance is a style of dance in which rhythmic sounds are produced by moving the feet. Shoes are worn with metal taps on the bottom, which produce the distinctive tap sound against the floor.

Tap dancing is believed to have been created by the blending of ". . . the Irish jig and the English clog with the Negro Shuffle."[13] Tap dancing, introduced in the minstrel shows, dominated the vaudeville shows of the late 1800s and remained popular well into the nineteenth century. It is a style of dance in which rhythmic sounds are produced by moving the feet. Shoes are worn with metal taps on the bottom, which produce the distinctive tap sound against the floor.

Although there are many prescribed tap dance steps, such as the "buck-and-wing," "shuffle," "flap step" and "cramp roll" (to name a few), tap dance is very improvisational. There are also many different styles of tap and tap dance performers. For example, "hoofers," such as Gregory Hines and Savion Glover, call attention to intricate footwork; "class acts," such as Fred Astaire and Ginger Rogers, execute steps in a refined manner, with elegant body movements; "flash acts," such as the Nicholas Brothers combine tap dance with acrobatic movements; and a dancer executing "soft shoe," such as vaudevillian George Primrose, would skim the floor and produce soft, muted steps.[14] Recent tap artists have developed other styles of tap, and older styles of past tap artists are being learned and practiced all the time.

Bill "Bojangles" Robinson (1879–1947) was one of the first of *many* African-American artists who popularized tap dance. Many remember Robinson as the person who tap danced with the child star Shirley Temple. Robinson, however, was a vaudeville tapper who first performed in 1891 at the age of twelve. He was also one of the first African-American performers to have regular employment in the mostly white theatre.

Sammy Davis, Jr. (1925–1990) was another African-American artist who popularized tap dance and was also first seen on the vaudeville stage as a child. Davis combined his dancing talents with his wonderful ability to sing and act and became one of America's most popular entertainers. Before his death, Davis starred in a movie entitled *Tap*, (1989) which brought about a new-found interest in tap dance by the general public.

Fred Astaire (1899–1987) and Ginger Rogers (1911–1995) made tap especially popular in musical theatre productions (see Figure 4.1). In addition to performing tap routines, they included ballroom dancing in their movies, bringing this unique combination of dance styles to the public. One famous movie musical in which they performed was *Top Hat* (1935), which contains many wonderful tap sequences. Gene Kelly (1912–1996), was another dancer who popularized tap dance. Known for his athletic ability, he presented tap dance in a very different manner from Astaire and Rogers, who were known for their gracefulness. His most famous tap dance can be seen in the movie *Singin' in the Rain* (1952), in which he actually does sing and tap dance in the rain.

Today, popular dancers like Savion Glover use tap dance in many endeavors, thus allowing audiences to view and appreciate this dance form. Tap dance legend Gregory Hines (1946–2003), starred in movies where tap sequences were highlighted. A movie entitled *White Nights* (1985, which also starred ballet great Mikhail Baryshnikov) features Hines in one of the most exciting tap dances ever to be captured on film. Hines also starred in the movie *Tap,* which featured some of the best known-tappers, such as Sammy Davis, Jr., Sandman Sims and the Nicholas Brothers.

Singer and dancer Paula Abdul also utilized tap dancing in her work, specifically in her music videos. These videos provided opportunities for younger audiences to view tap dance, thus increasing the popularity and visibility of this exciting dance form. More recently, Savion Glover developed choreography for the Broadway show *Bring in 'da Noise, Bring in 'da Funk* (1995), which mixes tap with hip-hop, break dancing and Glover's unique style.

SUMMARY

Jazz dance is an American art form whose roots can be traced back to Africa. Within the realm of jazz dance, we find a number of different styles, each one adding to the history of this popular dance form. Jazz dance, probably more than any other dance form, has reached across many cultural and socioeconomic boundaries and has thrilled the lives of all who see and participate in it.

Musical theatre and tap dance have been an important part of the American theatre and dance worlds. Seen on both the live stage and in movie musicals, these two dance forms have a historical and artistic link to jazz dance. Many artists from the jazz, ballet and modern dance worlds have contributed to the growth and development of these forms. These popular dance forms will continue to excite and entertain audiences for years to come. Table 4.1 details the characteristics of jazz dance, musical theatre dance, and tap dance. Table 4.2 details some major events in jazz dance, musical theatre, and tap dance.

Figure 4.1
Fred Astaire and Ginger Rogers in *Top Hat* (1935). Jerome Robbins Dance Division, The New York Public Library for the Performing Arts, Astor, Lenox and Tilden Foundations.

TABLE 4.1 CHARACTERISTICS OF JAZZ DANCE, MUSICAL THEATRE DANCE AND TAP DANCE

JAZZ DANCE	MUSICAL THEATRE DANCE	TAP DANCE
—Strong use of syncopated rhythms. —The repeated use of the plie. —The dancing has an improvisational feel. —Individual style is developed and demonstrated. —The dancing is presentational, visceral and sensual. —There is a strong use of varying dynamics. —Jazz dance can be seen on the theatrical stage, concert stage, and in movie musicals and popular music videos.	—Dance in musical theatre productions can be used to enhance the storyline and to move the storyline along. —Dance sequences can also stand alone as artistic works. —The script, music, lyrics and dance have a strong relationship. —Musical theatre dance can be seen on the theatrical stage and in movie musicals.	—Shoes are worn with metal taps on the bottom. —Rhythmic sounds are produced by moving the feet. —Tap dance has a strong use of syncopated rhythms. —Tap dance has a vocabulary with prescribed steps, but mostly, tap dance is improvisational. —There are different styles of tap and tap dancers: hoofers, class acts, flash acts, soft shoe, etc. —Tap dance can be seen on the theatrical stage, concert stage, and in movies, movie musicals and popular dance videos.

TABLE 4.2 OUTLINE OF JAZZ DANCE, MUSICAL THEATRE AND TAP EVENTS

17TH CENTURY	Slaves brought to America. Dancing and drumming is eventually seen on plantations.
1830s	Development of Minstrel shows. Whites perform in blackface.
1860	Blacks appear in Minstrel shows.
1866	One of the first musical theatre productions, *The Black Crook,* is presented.
1900s	Vaudeville, revue and burlesque shows begin. The Vaudeville era is a significant part of jazz dance history. Tap dance also becomes immensely popular during this time.
c.1919	Emergence of jazz music.
1921	Beginning of the Harlem Renaissance.
1921	First Negro musical performed, *Shuffle Along.*
1920s	Dance crazes such as the Charleston and the Black Bottom become popular.
1926	The musical *Peggy Ann* introduces the concept of connecting the script, music, lyrics and dance.
1935	Fred Astaire and Ginger Rogers appear in *Top Hat.*
1936	The Lindy, also known as the Jitterbug, becomes popular across America.
1943	Agnes de Mille choreographs *Oklahoma,* and presents dance numbers that not only help move along the storyline but also can stand alone as dramatic works. Agnes de Mille's work elevates the status of the musical theatre choreographer.
1955	Jack Cole, the father of jazz dance, choreographs *Kismet.*
1961	Jerome Robbins choreographs *West Side Story.*
1974	*A Chorus Line* opens on Broadway, with choreography by one of America's most popular musical theatre choreographers, Michael Bennett.
1981	*Cats* opens on Broadway.
1989	The movie *Tap* is made, starring Gregory Hines, Sammy Davis, Jr., the Nicholas Brothers, and Sandman Sims.
1991	The First American Jazz Dance World Congress, established by Gus Giordano, is held.
1995	*Bring in 'da Noise, Bring in 'da Funk* starring Savion Glover opens on Broadway.
1997	*The Lion King,* with choreography by modern dance choreographer Garth Fagan, opens on Broadway.
2000	*Aida,* with music by Elton John and Tim Rice, opens on Broadway.
2001	Mel Brooks's *The Producers* opens on Broadway.

Major Figures in Jazz Dance, Musical Theatre and Tap Dance

Jazz dance, including tap and musical theatre, are art forms that had their beginnings in America. Here is a partial list of artists that have had a major impact on this vernacular dance.

LEADING TO THE MINSTRELS AND BEYOND

JOHN DURANG (1768–1822)—Durang is known as one of America's first show dancers. Although he was white, he knew much about black dance. He was an expert at "hornpipe" dancing (a type of folk dance from England), although his version had many elements of African-American style. He was also the first white dancer to perform in blackface.

THOMAS RICE (1808–1860)—Better known as Daddy "Jim Crow" Rice, this performer was another white dancer who borrowed from the black culture. He made the song and dance number "Jump Jim Crow" immensely popular and it became a fad dance of the time. His performances paved the way for the minstrel shows to come.

WILLIAM HENRY LANE (1825–1852)—Better known as "Master Juba," Lane combined Irish jig and African movements in his dancing during the 1840s. Because he was black, he was not allowed to perform on stage with whites and performed for other blacks and Irish immigrants. He eventually became more popular than most white minstrel performers and toured with them for a while. He is also said to have influenced the tap dance movements created during his era.

GEORGE PRIMROSE (1852–1919)—A star of both the minstrel and vaudeville shows, Primrose popularized a style of tap dance known as the "soft shoe." The soft shoe is performed very gracefully, with the feet skimming, rather than loudly tapping, the floor.

THE VAUDEVILLE ERA

FLORENZ ZIEGFELD (1867–1932)—Ziegfeld was a producer who, in 1907, created the *Ziegfeld Follies*. The *Ziegfeld Follies* were a showcase of American "beauties," song and dance numbers and comedy routines. These shows were similar to the revues of the French *Folies Bergere*. Ziegfeld produced a new follies each year until the Great Depression of the 1930s.

NED WAYBURN (1874–1942)—Wayburn was one of the most famous dance directors of the vaudeville era. He also opened several dance studios that trained dancers for his shows. He focused on several types of show dancing, including musical comedy dancing, tap dance, ballroom, acrobats and modern ballet.

BILL "BOJANGLES" ROBINSON (1878–1949, see Figure 9.3)—One of the great tap dancers of the Vaudeville era, Robinson may be best remembered as the person who danced with Shirley Temple in the 1935 movie *The Little Colonel* and the 1938 movie *Rebecca of Sunnybrook Farm*. He was also one of the first black performers who presented artistic dance on the vaudeville stage. He had a graceful and delicate style that he perfected throughout his career of sixty years, which included work on Broadway and in movie musicals.

VERNON CASTLE (1887–1918) and **IRENE CASTLE** (1893–1969)—The Castles were a ballroom dance team introduced to the public by director Ned Wayburn. In addition to being dancers, they were also educators and introduced the public to ballroom dance through stage productions and classroom instruction. The Castles were immensely popular and set the standard for the way people dressed, acted and danced. They were in their heyday from 1912–1918. After Vernon's death, Irene continued to teach and even made educational dance films.

RAY BOLGER (1903–1987)—Best known as the actor who played the scarecrow in *The Wizard of Oz,* Bolger was one of vaudeville's best-loved stars. His specialty was comic dance and his long, lanky frame added to his comic ability.

MARGOT WEBB and **HAROLD NORTON**—Known as Norton and Margot, this duo was one of the few African-American ballroom dance couples of the Vaudeville era. Although they adopted a "white" dance vocabulary (or a dance style "reserved" for whites), they were not permitted to perform in the major vaudeville theatres. Nevertheless, their contribution to black dance and elevating the stature of the black artist has not gone unnoticed.

BROADWAY AND THE MOVIE MUSICAL

EUBIE BLAKE (1883–1983)—Blake was a composer and pianist who, together with other artists, created the Broadway musical *Shuffle Along* (considered to be the first "Negro" musical) in 1921. This production was popular with both white and black audiences and gave validity to the black Broadway artists.

ALBERTINA RASCH (1891–1967)—Originally a ballet dancer, Rasch was a dance director who helped to popularize "fancy dancing." Originally, fancy dancing was comprised of acrobatic tricks, high kicks, splits, etc. Rasch, however, used ballet movements and syncopated dance steps that were set to modern music. She directed a company called the *Albertina Rasch Girls,* who performed worldwide.

SEYMOUR FELIX (1894–1961)—Felix was also a dance director, but unlike Berkeley, he was concerned with the storyline of the musical. Beginning with the Rodgers and Hart musical *Peggy Ann,* produced in 1926, Felix was insistent that the dance numbers relate to or enhance the plot of the musical.

BOBBY CONNOLLY (1895–1944)—Another dance director of the 1920s, Connolly is best-known for his choreography in *The Wizard of Oz.* He is also credited with bringing "swing" dancing into popularity in musicals.

BUSBY BERKELEY (1895–1976)—Berkeley was a dance director known for his use of beautiful girls in his productions. Often the women in a Berkeley number were costumed to look exactly alike. He moved them around on stage in intricate patterns and provided audiences with aerial shots that produced a kaleidoscope effect.

ROBERT ALTON (1902–1957)—A popular dance director from the 1930s to the 1950s, Alton was fond of tap dance and employed it in several of his musicals, including *Anything Goes* and *Pal Joey.* Alton choreographed over thirty-two musicals.

JOSEPHINE BAKER (1906–1975)—Baker began her career during the Vaudeville era and eventually became a protégée of Eubie Blake. In 1925, she performed in Paris and became an instant success. In 1926, she performed at the *Folies-Bergere* and brought the jazz craze in Paris to an all-time high. She is credited with introducing such dances as the Charleston and the Black Bottom to the European audience.

THE MASTERS OF YESTERDAY AND TODAY

Several ballet and modern dance choreographers (previously discussed in ballet and modern "Major Figures") have created some of our best-loved jazz, tap and musical theatre choreography. For example: **GEORGE BALANCHINE** (*On Your Toes, I Married an Angel, Babes in Arms, The Boys From Syracuse, Song of Norway* and *Where's Charley?*), **AGNES DE MILLE** (*Oklahoma, Brigadoon, Carousel* and *Allegro*), **JEROME ROBBINS** (*On the Town, Fiddler on the Roof, High Button Shoes, West Side Story* and *The King and I*), **KATHERINE DUNHAM** (*Pins and Needles, Cabin in the Sky* and *Stormy Weather*), **HELEN TAMIRIS** (*Annie Get Your Gun, By the Beautiful Sea* and *Fanny*), **HANYA HOLM** (*Kiss Me Kate, Out of This World* and *My Fair Lady*), **VALERIE BETTIS** (*Beggar's Holiday*) and **TWYLA THARP** (remakes of *Hair* and *Singin' in the Rain*).

FRED ASTAIRE (1899–1987) and **GINGER ROGERS** (1911–1995)—One of America's most popular dancing couples, Astaire and Rogers combined tap, ballroom and ballet to create some of today's most memorable dance sequences. Rogers is said to have been a perfect partner to Astaire, who possessed a quality of grace and elegance in his movements. **HERMES PAN** (1910–1990), a Hollywood choreographer, frequently collaborated with Astaire to produce choreography for his dance sequences with Rogers, as well as his solo dances. The magic of Astaire and Rogers can be seen in such movies as *The Gay Divorcee* and *Top Hat.*

GENE KELLY (1912–1996, see Figure 9.4)—Kelly also combined tap, ballroom and ballet in his dancing. But unlike Astaire, Kelly was much more of a "physical" and acrobatic dancer. One of the most famous tap dance sequences known today was performed by Kelly in the movie *Singin' in the Rain.*

JACK COLE (1913–1974)—Cole began his career as a dancer with Denishawn and Humphrey-Weidman. The exposure to East Indian dance, introduced to him by Ruth St. Denis, had a lasting effect on him and his choreography became a mixture of jazz and world dance. One example of this unique hybrid is *Kismet,* which is one of Cole's most popular musicals.

FAYARD NICHOLAS (b. 1919) and **HAROLD NICHOLAS** (1924–2000)—Better known as the Nicholas Brothers, they were a tap dancing act that performed many acrobatic movements in their dance routines. They performed in such movies as *The Pirates* and *Stormy Weather.*

MICHAEL KIDD (b. 1919)—An outstanding musical theatre choreographer, Kidd won Tony Awards for his choreography in *Finian's Rainbow, Guys and Dolls* and *Can-Can.* One of his best-loved movie musicals is *Seven Brides for Seven Brothers,* with choreography that combines square dance, folk, ballet and modern with highly stylized acrobatic movements.

GOWER CHAMPION (1921–1980)—Before becoming a noted choreographer and director, Champion was a dancer and appeared in several musicals with his wife and dance partner, **MARGE** (b. 1923). As a director, he was an expert at "musical staging" which linked the acting and the dancing. Some of America's best-loved musicals that Champion choreographed and directed include *Bye Bye Birdie, Carnival, Hello, Dolly!, I Do! I Do!* and *42nd Street.*

CHARLES "HONI" COLES (1921–1992)—Coles is credited with creating high-speed rhythm tap and was known for his complex rhythmic patterns and movements. He was partnered with **CHARLES "CHOLLY" ATKINS** (1913–2003), who was known as a master of the soft shoe. Together they performed around the country for over twenty years, building their act into a comedy and dance routine. After their duet broke up, Coles and Atkins still performed sporadically for several years at benefits and reunion concerts. Atkins went on to become a choreographer for the groups at Motown Records. Coles was "rediscovered" in the late 1970s and choreographed on Broadway for performances such as *Bubbling Brown Sugar.*

LUIGI (b. 1925)—Another master teacher, Luigi, who is based in New York City, developed a technique and style that is uniquely his own and is studied by students all over the world. It includes the use of specific arm and hand positions, as well as shoulder, upper torso and hip movements.

SAMMY DAVIS, JR. (1925–1990)—Sammy Davis, Jr.'s career began as a young child, when he danced on the Vaudeville stage. Davis became a famous singer, dancer and actor and performed in all facets of the theatre—on Broadway, in movies, nightclubs, etc. He is considered one of the best tap dancers and all-around entertainers ever known in this country.

GWEN VERDON (1925–2000)—Trained in ballet, Verdon came to jazz dance after seeing Jack Cole perform. She worked with Cole for many years and was his assistant. She also worked with Michael Kidd, as well as Bob Fosse, whom she married. Also an outstanding actor and singer, Verdon appeared in several plays and movie musicals, including *Can-Can, Damn Yankees!, Redhead, Sweet Charity* and *Chicago.*

BOB FOSSE (1927–1987)—One of jazz dance's foremost choreographers, Fosse's choreography is recognizable by its angular shapes, undulating hip and shoulder movements, hip isolations and turned-in legs. Fosse has provided the choreography and direction for some of America's best-loved musicals: *Pippin, Cabaret, Chicago, Dancin',* and *Sweet Charity,* among others.

GUS GIORDANO (b. 1930)—One of today's leading jazz teachers, Giordano has recently developed the Jazz Dance World Congress, an organization created to preserve and expand the world of jazz dance. Based in Chicago, Giordano has had a jazz company and school since 1962.

CHITA RIVERA (b. 1933)—Rivera has appeared in the choreography of Michael Kidd, Jerome Robbins, Gower Champion and Jack Cole, to name a few. Her outstanding singing and acting ability has made her one of musical theatre's biggest stars. In 1992, she wowed audiences in the Broadway musical *Kiss of the Spider Woman*.

SHIRLEY MACLAINE (b. 1934)—For many years MacLaine was a "chorus girl." She eventually became one of the most famous dancing and acting stars. One of her most popular roles was in the movie version of *Sweet Charity*.

BRENDA BUFALINO (b. 1937)—Bufalino is the artistic director of the American Tap Dance Orchestra, one of the few dance companies that dedicate themselves exclusively to tap dance. Her choreography is complex, with movements that are syncopated and dynamic.

TOMMY TUNE (b. 1939)—Best known for his outstanding tap dance ability, Tune is also a choreographer and director, as well as a performer (one of the few artists who has been able to combine so many facets of the theatre into his working life). He has choreographed and directed some of Broadway's most popular shows, including *Best Little Whorehouse in Texas, A Day in Hollywood/A Night in the Ukraine, Cloud 9, My One and Only* and the re-make of *Bye Bye Birdie*.

MICHAEL BENNETT (1943–1987)—One of America's most famous Broadway choreographers, Bennett created one of Broadway's longest running musicals, *A Chorus Line*. He began dancing as a child and at the young age of twenty-three won a Tony Award for his choreography in *A Joyful Noise*. Several more Tony Awards were awarded to him throughout his career. Among his choreography and directing accomplishments are *Company, Follies* and *Dream Girls*.

GREGORY HINES (1946–2003)—Paired with his brother Maurice, Hines began tap dancing at a young age. Much of the resurgence of popularity that tap has enjoyed since the 1980s can be attributed to the many outstanding tap performances that Hines did. These performances can be seen in such movies as *White Nights* and *Tap*.

DANNY BURACZESKI (b. 1949)—One of today's most innovative jazz dance choreographers, Buraczeski studied ballet and modern dance before landing on Broadway. His choreography is directly linked to his use of jazz music, in that both are rhythmically and dynamically complex.

DEBBIE ALLEN (b. 1950)—Best known for her role on the television series *Fame,* Allen is not only an outstanding dancer but also one of today's best-known jazz dance choreographers (also one of the few women recognized in this field). With both television and Broadway experience, Allen is also respected as a director.

SAVION GLOVER (b. 1973)—As a child, Glover starred in *The Tap Dance Kid* on Broadway, which led to parts in other plays such as *Black and Blue* and *Jelly's Last Jam*. He also starred in the movie *Tap*, with Gregory Hines and Sammy Davis, Jr. Glover has since starred in and choreographed *Bring in 'da Noise, Bring in 'da Funk* on Broadway, which depicts the African-American struggle through tap, rap, hip-hop and funk

CHAPTER 5

Social Dance

INTRODUCTION

Most of the discussion up to this point has focused on professional concert dance. But just as folk dances provided entertainment for people in the sixteenth century, every era possesses styles of dancing that are performed purely for pleasure and entertainment. These dances are reflective of the cultures in which they exist.

BALLROOM AND POPULAR DANCE

Nearly every society has social dances that are a part of the culture. Each society has its own viewpoint about different aspects of social dance. For example, in some societies, social dance is a group activity and is meant to be enjoyed by an individual in conjunction with other people. In other societies, social dancing is meant to be enjoyed by two people—a couple (see Figure 5.1). Sometimes, social dance is seen as a completely individual activity. In some societies, strict rules apply to social dance with regard to males and females dancing together, appropriate physical contact and dancing in public. In other societies, dance is an accepted means of expression, and people of all ages and genders are encouraged to participate. Today in America, there are many different types of social dances (specifically ballroom and popular dances) and many different opinions regarding these dances.

Many social dances that were done in the past and are still done today in America came directly from the African-American communities and were adopted (and sometimes modified) by the white communities. For example, one of the most popular social dances ever developed was the Lindy-Hop. The Lindy-Hop was created in the Harlem nightclubs of the 1930s. Performed to swing music, it is a fast-paced, athletic dance done with a partner. When performed by the white community, this dance was usually done at a slower tempo and employed less of the daring lifts and tricks that were part of the original style. The Lindy-Hop paved the way for other couple dances, including the Jitterbug of the 1940s and even the

Every era possesses styles of dancing that are performed purely for pleasure and entertainment. These dances are reflective of the cultures in which they exist.

Nearly every society has social dances that are a part of the culture. Each society has its own viewpoint about different aspects of social dance.

Figure 5.1
Vernon and Irene
Castle, a famous
ballroom dance couple
of the early 1900s.
Jerome Robbins Dance
Division, the New York
Public Library for the
Performing Arts, Astor,
Lenox and Tilden
Foundations.

hustle of the late 1970s. It is interesting to note that these dance forms were almost always created by untrained dancers.

Although each decade has seen the development of specific dances, the focus of this chapter is on the period between the 1950s and the present in
America, a span of time in which a number of social dance styles emerged. For
example, in the conservative 1950s, ballroom dancing, which included dances

such as the waltz, fox trot and rumba, was a popular pastime for many Americans. Many of these styles of dance have their roots in European, African and South American movements. For example, the waltz was created in the nineteenth century and danced by the elite in England and Germany and eventually all across Europe, before it reached the United States. Other dances, such as the rumba, samba and tango, have their roots in movements created in the early 1900s in Africa and South America. In their original forms, these dances were considered to be too wild and sensual for the conservative communities. Therefore, some of the movements (especially hip movements) were changed and instead, balletic lifts and turns were added. These "refined" ballroom dances were performed almost exclusively by white dancers.

With the advent of rock and roll in the 1950s, the younger generation abandoned the prevailing conservative attitude. This attitude change, as well as the popularity of rock and roll music, resulted in the development of many new dances. Many African-American singers began to gain popularity, such as Little Richard and Chuck Berry, and white youths began to listen to the music of these singers, as well as mimic their dance movements. The most popular artist of that time, Elvis Presley, was a white singer who had a "soulful" quality to both his singing and his dancing. His hip-swaying movements were considered so offensive that he was only shown from the chest up on the popular "Ed Sullivan Show."

In 1960, Chubby Checker recorded "The Twist," and a new dance craze emerged. Other dances such as the Monkey, Mashed Potato and the Frug became popular with both black and white teenagers. The mid-1960s introduced radical performers such as Mick Jagger (of the Rolling Stones) and James Brown, both of whom had a unique dance style that their fans adored. In the late-1960s, a great change in dance styles occurred, which was a direct reflection of the attitudes of that time. The Vietnam War, the Civil Rights Movement and an increased interest in illegal drugs created the era sometimes referred to as "radical." Partner dancing, once the norm, was no longer the "in" thing to do and people danced alone or in groups. This type of dancing was known as "free-style" dancing. People wanted to "do their own thing," and this form reflected that feeling. A prime example of free-style dancing was captured in the film footage of Woodstock, a three-day rock music event held on a farm in upstate New York in the late 1960s. Here, people danced with ultimate abandonment, due largely in part to the overwhelming feeling of freedom, as well as an abundant supply of drugs.

In the 1970s, rock music was still going strong. A new style of music emerged in the late 1970s, however, that would again change the course of social dance. Disco music became the craze and popularized such dances as the Hustle and the Bus Stop. Partner dancing was also popularized during this period, largely due to the 1977 movie *Saturday Night Fever*, which starred John Travolta. This movie set the trend for what was to occur in popular dance for most of the late 1970s and early 1980s. Nightclubs, glamour and romance were the norm and looking fabulous was required of all who wanted to fit in.

Rap music was developed in the 1970s, but became most popular in the 1980s as a voice for inner-city minority groups. With this style of music came a new, popular form of dance known as hip-hop. Hip-hop, also known as "street dancing," combines several movements from African and jazz dance vocabularies with newly created movements. It was developed by untrained dancers, who continue to create new steps and combinations today. Although this discussion is not about professional or concert dance, it is interesting to note how popular dances (which begin at a raw level) are taken into the professional dance world and incorporated into videos, musical theatre productions and concert dance. For example, there are many music videos that incorporate hip-hop dancing and even popularize certain steps, such as the Running Man and the Roger Rabbit.

The fast-paced 1980s brought breakdancing to the mainstream and to the dance world.

Breakdancing actually became popular in the inner-cities during the 1970s, but did not receive widespread public attention until 1983, when the movie *Flashdance* featured a short breakdance section. Before going into the mainstream, gangs had been using breakdancing to settle differences, instead of fighting. Emphasis was placed on virtuosity; the one who could do the most interesting and difficult movements was the best.

The dancers who performed this highly physical and acrobatic form were known as B-Boys. Some believe that the "B" stands for breakdancing or breakin', while others believe that it stands for the Bronx, where it is said that breakdancing first developed. The B-Boys perfected this dance style and created movements such as "popping" and "locking." A typical breakdance session would be one where a circle is formed and each dancer enters the middle of the circle one at a time. Once inside the circle, the dancer demonstrates his or her best breakdance moves (obviously, B-Boys are males, but there are also B-Girls). Each dancer would do a short demonstration, sometimes lasting only a few seconds. Those few seconds, however, would be packed with fast and intricate footwork and amazing spins and flips.

Although we can look at hip-hop dancing and breakdancing as two different types of dance styles, it is important to note that breakdancing is part of the hip-hop culture. This culture has its roots in rap music, and all that rap music has inspired: a specific fashion trend; the emergence of graffiti art; a specific style of language/slang; and an importance placed on the DJ/emcee, who provides the rhythms, mixes, scratching and verbal "commands" that get the crowd going.

Another dance craze that was popularized in the early 1980s was slam dancing, in which the participants literally slammed into each other. Slam dancing was typically found in nightclubs that catered to the punk-rock crowd. This dance fad also began in the late 1970s (in England), but did not become popular with the mainstream in the United States until the 1980s (some feel as a direct revolt against the disco era). Later, there developed a small but dedicated crowd that took slam dancing one step further (by actually making it more violent). This dance craze, referred to as mosh dancing, was performed to heavy metal music. The participants referred to themselves as moshers, and religiously took part in this violent dance fad.

The early 1980s brought us music-television, and Michael Jackson was the first artist to present dance in a way that people had never previously witnessed. Jackson's *Thriller* video (1984, choreographed by musical theatre choreographer Michael Peters) was a sophisticated dance video that set a precedent for all other videos to follow. In order for a video to be popular, it had to contain unique, exciting and creative dance sequences. Since then, there have been many artists who regularly present dance in their videos, including Janet Jackson, Madonna, Britney Spears, Jennifer Lopez, Ricky Martin, and the list goes on and on. Many of the movements seen in these videos come from social dance forms, particularly hip-hop. There are also television stations who devote their entire programming to music videos and are extremely popular, two of which are MTV and VH-1.

Throughout the 1990s and into the twenty-first century, breakdancing and hip-hop have survived, and some would say, are still going strong. Today, there are many active B-Boy groups and B-Girl groups. Also, since the media has kept these styles in the forefront—in television commercials, on video stations, etc.—it is easy to see how it has remained so popular not only with the B-Boys/Girls but also in the mainstream.

Another dance craze to come into the twenty-first century is rave dancing, or raving. Danced to techno/electronic music, raving was for many years an underground dance style that began in the 1980s. Rave dancing is improvisational, with the participants strongly persuaded by the regular and hypnotic rhythm of the music. Many of the dance movements done at raves come directly from the hip-hop vocabulary, as does the use of the circle formation where the dancers "show their stuff." Also similar to hip-hop, there is a distinct style of dress that ravers wear, such as "phat pantz."

Raves can be held in a number of places, such as a nightclub. However, what some consider to be the "real" raves are the one-night, occasional parties set up in a warehouse or other space large enough to accommodate hundreds or even thousands of people. Although the mantra of most ravers is peace, freedom and friendliness, there is a dark side to many rave parties. The use of drugs, particularly Ecstasy, has led to a number of overdoses at these events. Since raves are so popular with U.S. youth, measures are being taken to make sure these events remain safe, such as promoters throwing drug-free raves and putting more of an emphasis on the music and the dancing, rather than the drug taking. The music and dancing, after all, are at the center of the raves and the main reasons why rave parties exist.

SUMMARY

Many people today, as in years past, enjoy social dancing. For example, there is now a tremendous interest in hip-hop and breakdancing. How long will this craze last? No one can know for sure. But one thing is certain: there will always be people who enjoy many aspects of social dancing and for a variety of reasons. Some feel that it is good exercise, while others say it makes them feel good on an emotional level. Many people dance to release their frustrations and negative energies and many people dance for the sheer fun of it. Whatever the reason people dance, the culture and society of the time to which they belong will certainly be reflected in the movements, style and music that make up the dance. Table 5.1 outlines some events in social dance.

TABLE 5.1   OUTLINE OF SOCIAL DANCE EVENTS

1920s	Beginning of the Harlem Renaissance. Dances such as the Charleston and the Black Bottom became popular (as discussed in *Chapter Nine*).
1930s	The Lindy Hop began in the black communities and was then adopted by the white communities.
1950s	Ballroom dancing came to the forefront. Dances such as the Waltz, Fox Trot and Rumba became very popular.
1950s	This decade saw the advent of rock and roll music. A new way of dancing was discovered.
1960s	Dances such as the Twist, Monkey and Mashed Potato emerged.
LATE 1960s	Dance styles emerged that reflected turbulent times. Free-style dancing became the popular form of social dance.
1970	Disco music brought about such dances as the Hustle and the Bus Stop. Partner dancing once again became popular.
1980s	Breakdancing, developed in the 1970s, became popular in the mainstream. Rap music gave rise to hip-hop culture. Slam dancing and mosh dancing were also seen in certain punk rock and heavy metal circles.
1980s	Music television (MTV, VH-1) popularizes the music video. Many social dance styles appeared in the videos of the music industry's most popular performers.
1990s–2000s	Rap music, hip-hop and breakdancing remain popular. Rave dancing, which began in the 1980s as an underground dance craze, became the popular dance form leading into the twenty-first century.

Dance Production: Behind the Scenes of a Dance Concert

INTRODUCTION

When an audience takes their seats in a theatre and the lights go down, a magical hush fills the air. The curtain goes up, the lights display splashes of color and the dance begins. The audience, concerned only with what is happening in the present, rarely thinks about the long process that has brought the dancers to this moment.

It would be surprising for some to realize exactly how much work and energy goes into mounting a dance production. An incredible amount of work has to be done in addition to creating the choreography and holding the rehearsals. This chapter discusses the steps that must be taken to produce a dance concert, and the people who play key roles in executing a production.

THE ARTISTIC DIRECTOR

No matter what the size of the company or the company's budget, having an outstanding *artistic director* is *crucial* to the success and survival of any dance company. The artistic director is responsible for the overall aesthetic and artistic vision of the company and makes decisions relative to all artistic issues.

One of the many responsibilities of the artistic director is to choreograph for the company or invite guest choreographers to make dances that will be performed in the company's repertoire. Companies that perform dances choreographed by someone other than the artistic director are usually known as repertory companies. Once it is determined which dances will appear on a concert, the artistic director "programs" the dances so that they are performed in an appropriate concert order. For example, beginning a concert with a dance that has a dark and dramatic theme might be too much for the audience to view as soon as they sit down in their seats. It might be more appropriate to begin a concert with a lighter dance, to allow the audience time to adjust to the concert setting. Similarly, the final dance of a concert should be one that will send the audience away with a lasting impression.

In addition to making artistic decisions, artistic directors sometimes also make business decisions, or at least give input into certain business issues. For example, dealing with touring and teaching schedules, financial concerns and

> *No matter what the size of the company or the company's budget, having an outstanding artistic director is crucial to the success and survival of any dance company.*

fund-raising efforts are all a part of the artistic director's job. They are also usually responsible for hiring (and sometimes firing) the dancers.

Most artistic directors are the "founders" of their dance companies. For example, Paul Taylor founded the Paul Taylor Dance Company in 1961 and still serves as its artistic director. There are, however, many people who have taken over the artistic directorship of an already existing company. Judith Jamison, for example, took over the artistic directorship of the Alvin Ailey American Dance Theatre after Ailey's death in 1990. Before a new director takes over an already existing company, decisions must be made as to whether or not he or she will continue to direct the company in the same artistic manner that the previous director had. In Jamison's case, there is a commitment to keeping the artistic vision and legacy of Alvin Ailey alive. Therefore, she directs the company with that intent and priority in mind. But for other companies, it might be determined (possibly by the Board members), that the new director should take the company in a different artistic direction that would benefit the dancers and the audience.

STEPS IN THE PRODUCTION PROCESS

Properly planning and organizing a dance concert is of the utmost importance. It is crucial that the organizers have a well thought-out plan of action and adhere to the timing and schedule of that plan. Of course, certain adjustments might have to be made if an emergency should arise (for example, problems with lighting equipment). In these cases, every effort should be made to fix problems as soon as possible. It is important to remember that many items have to be accomplished that cannot be put off until the last moment.

Properly planning and organizing a dance concert is of the utmost importance.

The beginning point in the process of producing a dance concert is deciding where the program will be performed. Assuming that the dance company has an operating budget, securing a space to conduct the concert (theatre, gymnasium, senior center, museum, etc.) is obviously important. Some companies have agreements to perform their home seasons in the same theatre every year, but many smaller companies rent out space on a concert-to-concert basis. Sometimes dancers have to perform in spaces that are less than ideal and many are willing to compromise in order to get the chance to perform. Compromising with regard to an adequate dance floor, however, may not be wise. Having the right kind of dance floor (preferably a sprung, smooth, wood floor) is important, since dancing on one that is not appropriate can be dangerous. For example, dancing on a floor that is too hard can lead to injuries such as shin splints, or ankle, knee and lower back problems. Other considerations for securing a space include: the availability of dressing room space; the stage size; available lighting; location of the space; the space's policies; and, of course, the cost.

Once a space is secured and rehearsals are underway, the artistic director, choreographer or any other person who may be responsible for the concert must direct their attention to factors including: publicity; designing and printing posters and programs; ticket sales; designing costumes; setting up lighting design(s); music (live or recorded); any sets and scenery; use of video or other technology; program order; and possibly renting equipment. In large, established companies, a number of people are responsible for accomplishing these tasks. Smaller dance companies who cannot afford to hire extra help are often left to take care of these details on their own. Therefore, in addition to creating the dances and running the rehearsals, the choreographer(s) or artistic director may also be responsible for most of the afore-mentioned tasks (with the dancers often pitching in as well). It is startling to see how many companies can successfully produce a concert, considering the enormous amount of work, effort and finances it takes to achieve this goal.

PEOPLE BEHIND THE PRODUCTION: THE SUPPORT STAFF

Few dance companies in the world can afford to have the ideal support and artis-tic staff. For the purposes of this discussion, let's create the ideal scenario and see who a dance company might employ if they had the funds to do so.

Few dance com-panies in the world can afford to have the ideal support and artistic staff.

The ideal dance company would have a hard-working, dedicated *Board of Directors*. This group primarily consists of prominent members of the business and artistic community, most of whom dedicate their time to the company with-out receiving any pay. One of the Board's main functions is to conduct fund-raising activities. Other functions may include establishing rules, regulations and policies regarding contracts, pay schedules, working conditions, etc. In some in-stances, the Board has the power to hire, fire and promote members of the artistic and support staff, including the dancers, choreographers and the artistic director.

In an ideal situation, a dance company would have a *business manager* as well as a *company director*. The business manager is in charge of the company's bud-get and may write grants and help with fund-raising efforts. Of course, he or she is also responsible for paying the bills and staff salaries. The company manager is more directly involved with the dancers and artistic director than the business manager is. He or she is responsible for designing rehearsal and production sched-ules and making sure everyone has the appropriate information to ensure that things run as smoothly as possible.

A well-known *public relations firm* can enhance the image of a dance com-pany immensely, while at the same time build an audience for the company. This firm is usually responsible for developing advertisements for newspapers, radio and television. They, along with a *graphics company*, also develop posters, flyers and the concert program. So many of today's successful advertisements depend on flashy and provocative visual images in order to capture the potential audience's attention. Dance companies that use photography in their advertisements can greatly benefit from these professional services.

A company needs a *box office manager*, who is in charge of reservations and ticket sales. A *house manager* is also required and is responsible for the ushers, seating arrangements, intermissions and anything else that might occur in the "house" of the theatre (as opposed to backstage).

Backstage, the *technical director* is in charge of all of the equipment and tech-nical aspects of the performance. Usually, this person has an *assistant technical director* and a *stage crew* to help with the technical work. The *stage manager* is responsible for "calling the show," or giving directions for the sound and lighting cues. This person works closely with the artistic director, technical director, and all the designers and assumes the majority of the responsibility once the performance gets underway. The stage manager's ability is crucial to the overall success of the performance. This person usually has an *assistant stage manager* who helps with details. The stage manager also works closely with the *lighting board operator(s), follow spot operator(s)* and *sound board operator(s)*, who, under his or her direction, "run" the show, usually from the lighting and sound booths.

In addition to the above mentioned positions, some dance companies might also have *legal counsel; insurance agents; dance injury specialists* and *massage therapists; financial administrators; marketing directors; out-reach coordinators; residency and workshop coordinators; rehearsal assistants; school directors; secretarial staff;* and *travel/booking agents.*

With the great variety of dance companies in the world, there are almost certainly some positions that have not even been mentioned that may in fact be a major part of some companies. It is striking, however, to look at the broad spectrum of dance companies—from the large, well-established companies to the small and struggling ones—and see how they are all committed to producing dance concerts and sharing them with the public.

THE ARTISTIC COLLABORATORS

Several other people are important to the artistic development and production of a dance concert. In an ideal situation, a company would have a *lighting designer, costume designer, costume construction crew, hair and makeup artist* and *set and scenery designer*. They might also have a *musical director* and *composer(s)* and even an *orchestra* associated with the company.

THE LIGHTING DESIGNER

In smaller, lower-budget companies, the collaboration with the lighting designer usually takes priority over all other factors, leaving the artistic director, dancers, etc., to design and make costumes, do their own hair and makeup and work with previously recorded music. One of the main reasons why this collaboration is so important to the production is because the lights provide a theatrical feel to the dance that most choreographers desire. This statement does not imply that dances cannot be performed in natural light (or even under fluorescent lights!), but lighting can help transform the stage space and help choreographers "say" what they want. "Light itself is mysterious, inseparable from what it makes visible. In the natural world, though light fosters sight, it is neutral on matters of meaning. Theatrical light, entirely unnatural, fosters sight and insight; it is a subliminal whisper, providing emphasis, telling us what to make of what we see."[1]

Another reason why lighting designers are so valuable to most dance companies is because these designers not only have the artistic sense needed to create the designs, but they also possess the essential practical knowledge regarding electricity, lighting instruments, use of color, light plots and the technical aspects of the theatre. Although some choreographers can design lights for their own dances, most have neither the time nor the knowledge of design, as well as the equipment, to properly light a concert.

Part of the knowledge that a lighting designer must have involves the different pieces of lighting equipment. A designer has many types of lighting instruments that he or she uses to create the desired effects on the stage. See Figure 6.1, which shows universal lighting symbols. Many lighting designers also utilize special software that have instrument and manufacturer specific symbols. For example, a *fresnel* is a type of spotlight that features a lens with an edged or stepped pattern. This lens is a thick piece of glass patterned on the inside to resemble a series of steps. This design gives the light "a wide spread of illumination—which creates an even field with soft edges . . ."[2] An *ellipsoidal spotlight* is used when

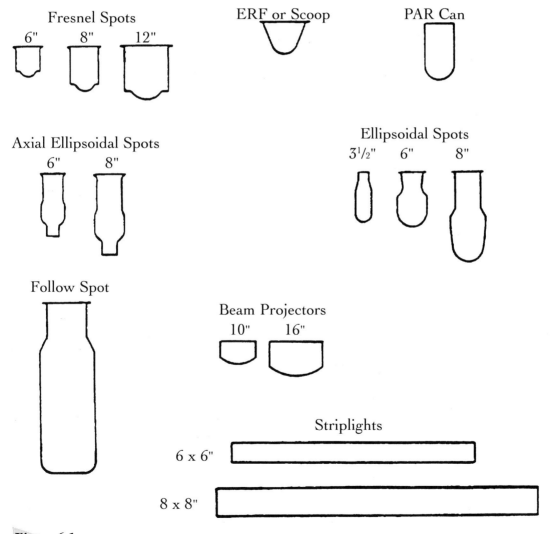

Figure 6.1
Lighting Instruments, ½" scale. These symbols are recognized by the United States Institute for Theatre Technology as universal symbols.

the designer wishes to project a sharper, more focused beam of light. This instrument uses an "ellipsoidal reflector," a bowl-shaped apparatus that sits behind and around the bulb (or "lamp") and casts all the light forward. Additionally, the ellipsoidal spotlight has metal shutters that can be manipulated to precisely control the spill of the light and the relative sharpness or softness of the beam's edge. There is also an *ellipsoidal reflector floodlight* (also known as an ERF or "scoop"), which can be used for ". . . throwing a broad wash of light over a wide area."[3] Often times, this instrument is used for lighting scenery. A *PAR can* or *PAR head* (parabolic aluminized reflector) provides an ". . . oval-shaped beam of light . . . [which] is uniquely harsh, [while] the beam edge is fairly soft."[4] Designers use these four commonly known lighting instruments in different ways in order to produce certain "looks" on stage. The designer can use them separately or in conjunction with one another.

Lighting designers also use *striplights* to create a wash of light on a backdrop, cyclorama or scrim (set pieces or pieces of material that hang in the upstage part of the stage). *Follow spots* are lighting instruments that are not found directly on the stage, but are projected onto the stage by an operator who is usually a far distance away (such as at the back of the theatre or in the lighting booth). The operator can move the beam of light all around the stage area. The follow spot can produce either a sharp or diffused light and the beam of light can be made very small or large. This instrument is usually used to highlight a person or object on stage. Another lighting instrument designers use is a *beam projector,* which throws a sharp beam of light and is often used to create special effects, such as sunlight coming in through a window.

There are also *automated lighting instruments* (also known as *movable lighting instruments* or *intelligent lighting instruments*), which can project many different patterns and produce many different effects. These instruments are fully computerized and have special features such as color changers. Technological advancements in theatrical lighting, such as these movable instruments, give lighting designers a whole new range of possibilities.

Of course, all these lighting instruments must be strategically placed on the stage. In dance, many designers will use the primary light source from the sides of the stage because this use of light makes the dancers look more three dimensional. The designer drafts all these lighting instruments onto a *light plot* (a blueprint of where the instruments will hang in the theatre). The lights are then hung and focused to specific areas on the stage. The lighting designer often uses different colored *gels* in front of the lighting instruments to produce certain effects. For example, if a dance depicted a person who is in a panicked state, the designer may choose to have an intense red glow over the stage. On the other hand, if the dance was about a mother's love for her child, the designer might illuminate the stage with a warm, pink, rosy color. Designers may also incorporate the use of a *gobo,* which is a small, flat piece of metal with a cut-out pattern in it. Gobos can produce many effects, such as a starry night, a cityscape or a forest filled with trees, to name a few. High-quality glass gobos, called *lithos,* can accommodate precise, fine-detailed images, such as photographs or line drawings, and can also be in color or black and white. These *lithos* pass light very effectively and, depending on the pattern, can create everything from a beautiful, soft-shaded effect to multicolored projections.

Before the lighting designer begins to design the light plot, one or more meetings usually take place with the choreographer. The designer may also come to rehearsal(s) and watch the dance or dances that he or she will create designs for, or "light." Several items are usually discussed and taken into consideration when the designs are made, including: costume color; set design (if any); whether or not the dance will incorporate slides, film or video; whether any special effects will be required; and, most important, the choreographer's concept of the dance. Although some choreographers and lighting designers work independently from each other, many designers desire the aforementioned information in order to make the most effective lighting design.

One of today's most popular and sought-after lighting designers is Jennifer Tipton (b. 1938). She has designed lights for both dance and theatre and has worked with such choreographers as Paul Taylor, Twyla Tharp and Jerome Robbins. She has won many awards for her designs, including two Tony Awards, two Drama Desks awards and an Obie. What makes her such an outstanding designer is her ability to use light to ". . . [move] a piece along onstage. She knows how to punctuate movement in light, [and] create a narrative line for the action."[5] With her lighting designs, she is able to get the audience to see what she wants them to see. Although there are several different ways to light dance, Tipton relies on her intuition, stating, "There are many ideas. They're all light ideas. There's white light. There's colored light. There's light along the walls. There's light from the front. There's light from the side. There's light that lights the head. I'm playing with all of those things and I'm responding with my gut."[6]

THE COSTUME DESIGNER

Although many times dancers perform in "typical" dancewear, such as leotards and tights, costumes designed specifically for a dance can enhance the theatrical feel of that dance and also provide information to the audience regarding character, time period and mood. The process that occurs between the choreographer and the costume designer is similar to the one that occurs between the choreographer and the lighting designer (i.e., meetings, discussions, viewing the dances). In addition, the choreographer usually has the opportunity to view sketches of the costumes before the construction gets underway.

One of the most important issues concerning costumes has to do with mobility. The dancer(s) must be able to move comfortably in the costume. It also cannot detract from any of the movements found within the choreography. Therefore, it is very important that the dancers get a chance to rehearse in the costumes, so that adjustments can be made if necessary.

Many types and styles of costumes can be designed for dance concerts. Most designers (sometimes with input from the choreographer) decide whether the costumes will be realistic, abstract, pedestrian, historical or "period," dancewear-like, etc. Decisions must also be made on the appropriate color or colors that will be used and if it is important that the color be significant to the theme of the dance. The material used must also be considered, since costumes have to "flow" and "move" in the right ways.

Once the designs are sketched out, it is often up to the costume construction crew to "build" the costume. The designer may be a part of this crew, however,

One of the most important issues concerning costumes has to do with mobility. The dancer(s) must be able to move comfortably in the costume.

some designers do not even know how to sew. In this case they serve as overseers of the construction, take part in the costume fittings and make suggestions for alterations.

Although the general public does not know most costume designers, several famous designers from the fashion world have designed for major choreographers. For example, Ralph Lauren, Oscar de la Renta, Norma Kamali and Isaac Mizrahi have all designed costumes for dances choreographed by Twyla Tharp. Martha Graham also worked with fashion designers; Halston having been one of her favorites.

The costume designer may also be responsible for determining how the dancer's hair will be worn and what makeup he or she will wear. In some companies, hair and makeup artists assist the dancers, but in most companies, the dancers are responsible for doing their own makeup and hair styles.

THE SET AND SCENERY DESIGNER

Today, as in the past, artists from different genres collaborate on many projects that blend different art forms together in unique and interesting ways. For example, choreographers and visual artists have been collaborating on set designs since the court dances of the sixteenth century. As we have seen, classical ballet always employs the use of elaborate scenery. Similarly, choreographers in other dance genres have worked with set and scene designers and have produced outstanding works of art.

One long-term collaboration that has a place in modern dance history is the one between modern dance legend Martha Graham and the Japanese-American sculptor Isamu Noguchi (1904–1988). Graham and Noguchi collaborated on projects for more than fifty-three years. The ". . . process [they employed] was fairly uncomplicated. It would begin with Graham talking with the sculptor about the idea or theme for a piece. Noguchi would then make a tiny mock-up of the set. . . . The choreographer would seldom suggest any changes in the design; if something didn't quite work, she would make adjustments in her own work."[7] Obviously, these two artists had a wonderful working relationship, producing some of the most outstanding dances, set pieces and designs known in the modern dance world. Some of Graham's dances that include set design and set pieces created by Noguchi are *Appalachian Spring, Night Journey* and *Errand Into the Maze.*

COMPOSERS AND MUSICIANS

Many choreographers are now choosing to create dances that utilize some of today's technological advancements.

As stated earlier, some dance companies have a musical director and orchestra associated with it, although this association is usually found only in large ballet companies. Most dance companies that want to collaborate with live musicians do so on "special" occasions, which usually means when money is available. It should be noted that grants are sometimes available for collaborative projects. In recent years, however, the dollar amount given by many grant organizations has been cut dramatically.

Throughout the history of dance, several collaborations between musicians and choreographers proved to be outstanding successes. Several have already been mentioned, such as the collaborations between composer Igor Stravinsky and ballet choreographers Vaslav Nijinsky and George Balanchine, and the many collaborations between composer John Cage and modern dance choreographer Merce Cunningham. The marriage of movement and music is a natural and important one, and many choreographers would prefer to work with live musicians (as opposed to recorded music). Most choreographers, however, end up working with previously recorded music because of financial constraints.

OTHER COLLABORATIONS

Many choreographers are now choosing to create dances that utilize some of today's technological advancements (see Figure 6.2). With the advent of technology came the desire, for some choreographers, to go beyond "traditional" dance making and to experiment with the highly sophisticated film, video, computer systems and lighting equipment that is available. Therefore, the demand for film makers, videographers and computer experts in dance has increased. Like everything else, however, finances are a large issue, especially since most of the equipment needed to do a multi-media (or mixed-media) project is very expensive. Some choreographers, in an attempt to save money, have learned how to use much of the equipment themselves and then rely on renting or borrowing it in order to complete their projects.

It should be mentioned that the use of video, CD and DVD, even at the most simplistic level, is important to most choreographers. For choreographers, recording their dances on video, CD or DVD is the only way to truly preserve a dance. Because dance is an ephemeral art and is only alive at the moment that it is being performed, having a dance videotaped keeps a record of it, either for future use or merely to have in a person's archives.

SUMMARY

The task of producing a dance concert is an overwhelming and exhausting one, especially for the smaller companies that have to do most of the work themselves. The process can be less complicated if the production efforts and the people involved are organized and stick to a clearly outlined plan. Of course, money is always a concern in dance production and keeping within a set budget is often difficult. Choreographers and artistic directors can sometimes supplement their budgets with grants from public and private sources, although the grant process can be a tedious and competitive one. Many dance companies, both large and small, have scaled down their production efforts (in terms of the amount of concerts done each year and the dollar amount allotted for each production) in order to save money and keep ticket prices reasonable.

Although the future looks challenging for many dance companies, the passion and love for dance that most artistic directors and company members share has been the sustaining force that keeps many companies alive. One day, more value may be placed on the arts and substantial funding may be available for these outstanding artists.

The task of producing a dance concert is an overwhelming and exhausting one.

Figure 6.2
Vera's Body, created by Troika Ranch, a company that utilizes dance technology. Copyright © by Tom Brazil.

Modern Dance

MODERN DANCE

When compared to ballet, modern dance is relatively new, beginning in the late 1800's and early 1900's. Modern dance evolved as a direct revolt against the restrictions of ballet. Modern dance is an art form that continues to evolve in order to express contemporary situations rather than fairy-tales of classical ballet.

Isadora Duncan (1862–1928) is the "Mother of modern dance." She believed that movements should be drawn from nature. The "Duncan technique" was made up of movements like hopping, skipping, running, and leaping. She wanted to free the body from the confines of ballet. Duncan liked to dance in sheer tunics and barefoot. She found great popularity for her style in Europe. She was quite flamboyant and eccentric. She led an unorthodox life by rejecting the common morality of her time.

Ruth St. Denis (1878–1968) began choreographing after seeing an advertisement with the Egyptian goddess Isis in it. She took interest in exotic dance styles from Egypt and India. She performed these dances on the Vaudeville circuit. St. Denis married Ted Shawn (1891–1968) in 1914 and together they founded Denishawn, a dance company that toured the United States. When their marriage failed in the 1930's, Shawn established Jacob's Pillow, a school in Massachusetts. This was designed as an all male dance company and still exists today.

Doris Humphrey (1895–1958) and Charles Weidman (1901–1975) trained with Denishawn but left in 1928 to found the Humphrey-Weidman School and Dance Company. They also developed a technique based on fall and recovery with a strong emphasis on balance and the pull of gravity. Their student José Limon (1908–1972) was a Mexican-American choreographer and dancer. One of his most famous works is *The Moor's Pavane* (1949).

Martha Graham (1894–1991), also a Denishawn student, established the Martha Graham School of Contemporary Dance in 1927. This company also exists today. Martha Graham is arguably the single most influential figure in American modern dance. Originally she established an all female company but eventually male dancers were incorporated. Many of her dances were psychological dramas that were primarily based on themes drawn from Greek mythology, American pioneers, and American Indians. Her dance techniques were based on a system of contraction and releases of the center of the body. She was the type of artist who saw new possibilities for expression outside her artistic background. She rebelled against the dance styles of the times by using a flexed foot as well as an extended foot, using parallel positions of the feet and legs as well as turned out positions. Graham created 181 works, and in 1976 received the Medal of Freedom, the highest civilian honor in the United States.

Other influential figures include:

Eric Hawkins (1909–1994) was a student of Balanchine's. He choreographed for Ballet Caravan (NYC Ballet). Hawkins became Graham's first male dancer. He later founded his own company and school in 1951. His technique was "free flow" based on fluid, effortless movements.

Katherine Dunham's (1909–2006) first dance is entitled *Negro Rhapsody* and was performed in 1931. She is best known for combining native Caribbean and modern dance forms. She appeared in musical theater and movie musicals. Her rhythmic style was also influential on Jazz dance.

Alwin Nikolais (1912–1993) used dance as motion rather than an emotion. Nik's dances are called "non-literal" and abstract. His dance theater works blend his skills as a choreographer, composer, set designer, lighting designer, and costume designer.

Alvin Ailey (1931–1990) was born in Texas and was largely influenced by his upbringing there where they worked in the fields. He trained as a dancer on the west coast, where he was influenced by the style of Katherine Dunham. Ailey developed his own company in New York in the mid 1950's called Alvin Ailey Dance Theatre. He combined modern, jazz, and world dance to create a unique style. It is still a world renowned company. One of his most acclaimed dances is called *Revelations* (1960). This dance depicts the religious heritage of the African-American and is set to negro spiritual music. At his death, Judith Jamison took over as director of the company.

POST MODERN

The "father" of post modern dance is Merce Cunningham (1919–). He danced with Martha Graham for five years. He developed Merce Cunningham Dance Company in 1953. His trademark is dance events which use "chance and indeterminacy" to arrange movements. He is also known for collaborating with the avant garde composer John Cage and artist Robert Rauchenberg.

Paul Taylor (1930–) studied under Graham, Humphrey, Limon, and Cunningham. His style is innovative yet approachable. In one famous piece, *Duet* (1957), he and the pianist did not move for the entire piece. In response, the critic Louis Horst gave the performance a blank review space in *Dance Observer*.

Twyla Tharp (1942–) grew up in California, where her parents ran a drive-in movie. This exposed her to American popular culture, setting the backdrop for her future work. Tharp studied modern dance with Graham, Nikolais, Cunningham, and Taylor, but soon set out on her own as a choreographer. In 1973, Robert Joffrey invited her to work with his company, where she choreographed the highly successful *Deuce Coupe* (1973) set to the music of the Beach Boys. Another huge success was created specifically for Mikhail Baryshnikov with the American Ballet Theatre. This piece is entitled *Push Comes to Shove* (1976). Tharp also did the choreography for several films including: *Hair*

(1979), *Ragtime* (1981), *Amadeus* (1984), and *White Knights* (1985), starring Baryshnikov and the tap dancer Gregory Hines.

Ulysses Dove (1947–1996) was born in Columbia, South Carolina. He danced with Cunningham before becoming a principal in Alvin Ailey's company in 1980. He created works for many companies, including *Red Angels* (1994) and *Twilight* (1996) for the New York City Ballet.

Bill T. Jones (1952–) is a choreographer who takes on controversial material such as homosexuality and racism. He met his life partner and collaborator Arnie Zane while in college. They formed the Bill T. Jones/Arnie Zane Dance Company. After Zane's death from AIDs, Jones took on the subject of terminal illness. This caused a debate in the dance world when the critic Arlene Croce labeled it "victim art."

JAZZ, MUSICAL THEATER, TAP DANCE AND HIP HOP

The history of Jazz dance can be traced back to Africa. When the slaves were brought to America, they brought their music and dance forms. Eventually these dances were showcased in the theaters. Beginning in the 1830s, the "Minstrel Shows" showcased black songs and dances.

The Vaudeville era was also significant to jazz dance history. It was a time when jazz and tap flourished and also marked the emergence of jazz music. Vaudeville included short songs and dances collected as an ensemble for entertainment. Bill "Bojangles" Robinson and Sammy Davis, Jr. were popular child dancers during this era. The Harlem Renaissance was another important time period for jazz dance. Black singers and dancers performed in many exclusive clubs in Harlem for the high society. The popularity of the dances seen in these clubs caused a dance craze which spread around the world. This time period in America came to be known as the Roaring Twenties. Some of the most popular dances of this decade were the Charleston and the Black Bottom. "Flappers" were women who wore short, fringed dresses and danced the Charleston.

Many consider Jack Cole to be the father of jazz dance. He developed a style in the 1940s that is still seen in today's jazz choreography. Bob Fosse (1927–1987) is one of jazz dance's most famous choreographers. He is also known for his choreography in some of America's most loved musicals, such as *Chicago, Sweet Charity* and *Caberet*.

American Musical theatre has its roots in all forms of dance. Dance in musical theater productions can be used to enhance the storyline and move the plot along. In 1943, Agnes de Mille, a pioneer of musical theatre choreography, choreographed *Oklahoma!*, in which dance was used for the first time in a fully integrated way in the telling of the story. Her work helped musical theatre choreographers get the respect they deserved. Another famous musical theatre choreographer is Jerome Robbins (1918–1998). He choreographed the popular *West Side Story* (1957). Susan Stroman is a choreographer and director. In 1999, she helped to create and direct *Contact*, a highly acclaimed dance theatre work. She also directed and choreographed the successful musical *The Producers* in 2001.

TAP DANCING

Tap dancing is a style of dance in which rhythmic sounds are produced by moving the feet (shoes are worn with metal taps on the bottom). There are a variety of steps and styles in tap dance. "Flash Acts" combine tap dance with acrobatic movements. "Hoofers" call attention to intricate footwork. "Class acts" execute steps in a refined manner, with elegant body movements.

IMPORTANT FIGURES IN TAP DANCE

Bill "Bojangles" Robinson (1925–1990) was one of the great tap dancers of the Vaudeville era. He is remembered for many performances, including his dancing with Shirley Temple in the movie *Rebecca of Sunnybrook Farm*.

Sammy Davis, Jr. (1925–1990) is another dancer whose career spanned most of the 20th century. He was a famous singer, dancer and actor who achieved popularity in the Las Vegas nightclub circuit among other places.

Fred Astaire (1899–1987) and Ginger Rogers (1911–1995) were one of America's most popular dancing couples. They combined tap, ballroom and ballet to create some of the most memorable dance sequences in movies and musicals. Astaire was a choreographer, tap dancer, actor and singer who began his career by dancing on the Vaudeville circuit with his sister Adele.

Gene Kelly (1912–1996) was also known for combining tap, ballroom, and ballet in his dancing. He is famous for his role in the movie *Singing in the Rain* (1952) which he co-directed with Stanley Donen, a dancer/choreographer/director from Columbia, South Carolina.

Gregory Hines (1946–2003) began dancing at an early age with his brother Maurice and with their father. He danced at the famous Apollo Theatre in Harlem and went on to star on Broadway and in movies and television series. Two of his well-known movies are *White Nights* (1985) with Mikhail Baryshnikov and *Tap* (1989) with Sammy Davis, Jr. and Savion Glover among others.

Savion Glover (1973–) starred as a child in *The Tap Dance Kid* on Broadway. He is also known for his choreography in the Broadway show *Bring in da Noise, Bring in da Funk* (1996), which mixes hip hop, breakdancing and his unique style.

HIP HOP

Hip Hop refers to a dance style that evolved on the streets. In particular, it began in the 1970s and 1980s as "breakdance" and involved improvisation by the performers. Today, many dance instructors include hip hop as part of their dance curriculum.

SOCIAL DANCE

STEP DANCE

Step dance is the term for dance in which footwork is the most important component. One form is Irish Step Dance, where the upper body is held in a rigid position while the feet perform intricate steps. Michael Flatley choreographed *Riverdance* (1995), which popularized Irish Step Dance.

Another form of step dancing, "stepping," has its roots in Africa and is performed by African American fraternities and sororities. Group routines are often performed in competitions between the fraternities and sororities in "Step Shows." These dances are highly choreographed and involve clapping, stomping and may make use of props such as canes or sticks. The film "Stomp the Yard" (2007) featured stepping.

BALLROOM DANCE

While ballroom dance has recently become popular because of television shows such as "Dancing with the Stars," ballroom dance has long been enjoyed both socially and competitively.

In the American style of dances, there are two categories: smooth and rhythm. In the smooth dances, the couples are seen to move all around the dance floor. The costumes for these dances usually involve full gowns for the ladies and formal wear for the men. These smooth dances include the Waltz, Tango, Foxtrot, and Viennese Waltz.

Rhythm dances are more often performed more or less in one spot, and the women are often dressed in short skirts to emphasize the legs, while the men might wear tightly fitted shirts and pants. The American rhythm dances include the Cha-cha, Rumba, East Coast Swing, Bolero and Mambo.

One form of social dance that has gained great popularity is the Carolina Shag, which developed along the beaches of North and South Carolina. It is a form of swing dance performed to "beach music," and it is the state dance of South Carolina. There are several organizations which promote friendly competition among shaggers of all levels.

IN CONCLUSION

Dance had its origins from the early age of man as he used his body as a means of communication. Through the ages, dance became increasingly formalized as we see the development of courts ballets, which gave rise to the Romantic Era in France, to the Classical Era of Russia, to Contemporary dance. This movement gave way to the development of dance in America in the 20th century.

Many genres of dance have developed including ballet, modern, hip hop, jazz, tap and ballroom. Dance is all around us, and it is important to develop an understanding and appreciation of it.

EVALUATION SHEETS

GUEST SPEAKER EVALUATION

From time to time, a guest lecturer will be invited to speak about a relevant topic. Guest choreographers, lighting directors, performance arts managers, stage managers, musicians, make-up artists and costumers might share information with the class. Please use this form to evaluate the material provided by each guest speaker.

Who is the guest speaker?

What is his or her area of expertise?

Where is the guest speaker employed?

What is his or her educational background?

What kind of experience have they had in their careers?

How long have they been in their profession, and have they made any career changes within their profession?

List five things that you learned from this guest lecturer.

GUEST SPEAKER EVALUATION

From time to time, a guest lecturer will be invited to speak about a relevant topic. Guest choreographers, lighting directors, performance arts managers, stage managers, musicians, make-up artists and costumers might share information with the class. Please use this form to evaluate the material provided by each guest speaker.

Who is the guest speaker?

What is his or her area of expertise?

Where is the guest speaker employed?

What is his or her educational background?

What kind of experience have they had in their careers?

How long have they been in their profession, and have they made any career changes within their profession?

List five things that you learned from this guest lecturer.

GUEST SPEAKER EVALUATION

From time to time, a guest lecturer will be invited to speak about a relevant topic. Guest choreographers, lighting directors, performance arts managers, stage managers, musicians, make-up artists and costumers might share information with the class. Please use this form to evaluate the material provided by each guest speaker.

Who is the guest speaker?

What is his or her area of expertise?

Where is the guest speaker employed?

What is his or her educational background?

What kind of experience have they had in their careers?

How long have they been in their profession, and have they made any career changes within their profession?

List five things that you learned from this guest lecturer.

GUEST SPEAKER EVALUATION

From time to time, a guest lecturer will be invited to speak about a relevant topic. Guest choreographers, lighting directors, performance arts managers, stage managers, musicians, make-up artists and costumers might share information with the class. Please use this form to evaluate the material provided by each guest speaker.

Who is the guest speaker?

What is his or her area of expertise?

Where is the guest speaker employed?

What is his or her educational background?

What kind of experience have they had in their careers?

How long have they been in their profession, and have they made any career changes within their profession?

List five things that you learned from this guest lecturer.

GUEST SPEAKER EVALUATION

From time to time, a guest lecturer will be invited to speak about a relevant topic. Guest choreographers, lighting directors, performance arts managers, stage managers, musicians, make-up artists and costumers might share information with the class. Please use this form to evaluate the material provided by each guest speaker.

Who is the guest speaker?

What is his or her area of expertise?

Where is the guest speaker employed?

What is his or her educational background?

What kind of experience have they had in their careers?

How long have they been in their profession, and have they made any career changes within their profession?

List five things that you learned from this guest lecturer.

DANCE PERFORMANCE REVIEW

You are required to attend several dance concerts as a class requirement, because it is through the observation of live performances that you will begin to have an appreciation for dance. As you watch **each** piece within each performance, please use this form to answer the questions listed below. Answer every question about each dance that you watch, and turn in these reviews at the class immediately following the performance.

Choreography—Who is the choreographer of the piece? What style or genre of dance is being performed? What is the choreographer trying to accomplish? Is he or she telling a story, or is the dance simply abstract, with no story line? What patterns may be observed? Is the entire stage used, with movements to both stage left and right, and both upstage and downstage? Or do the dancers remain somewhat stationary, with little movement across the stage? Was the choreographer successful in engaging your attention and appreciation?

The Dancers—Observe the performance of the dancers themselves. Are they professionals, amateurs, or student performers? Are they rehearsed and prepared for the performance? Are they cast appropriately for the role they are dancing? Look at the number of dancers on stage. Are there solo performers? Do they perform as a duo, or a pas de deux (step of two)? Are there both male and female dancers, and how do they interact?

The Lighting—Look at the colors of lighting that has been selected. Were "warm" tones, such as yellows or reds used, or were "cool" tones such as greens or blues selected? What lights were used (for example, spot lights, head lights, shin lights?)

Set/scenery—Describe the scenery. Was there a painted backdrop, or was a simple "cyc" that was lit used? What props, if any, were used? Describe the scenery in detail.

Costumes/Make-up—What type of costume was used? What colors and fabrics were selected? Is elaborate make-up used, or simple stage make-up for the dancers? Describe the types of shoes (if any) worn by the dancers.

Music—Is the music recorded, or is it being performed by live musicians or an orchestra? Is the music classical, or is it more discordant, or even computer generated? Consider how the music works with the choreography.

Overall impression—Did you enjoy the performance? Describe your reactions to the piece.

NAME _____

SECTION NUMBER _____   STUDENT ID NUMBER _____

DANCE PERFORMANCE REVIEW

You are required to attend several dance concerts as a class requirement, because it is through the observation of live performances that you will begin to have an appreciation for dance. As you watch **each** piece within each performance, please use this form to answer the questions listed below. Answer every question about each dance that you watch, and turn in these reviews at the class immediately following the performance.

Choreography—Who is the choreographer of the piece? What style or genre of dance is being performed? What is the choreographer trying to accomplish? Is he or she telling a story, or is the dance simply abstract, with no story line? What patterns may be observed? Is the entire stage used, with movements to both stage left and right, and both upstage and downstage? Or do the dancers remain somewhat stationary, with little movement across the stage? Was the choreographer successful in engaging your attention and appreciation?

The Dancers—Observe the performance of the dancers themselves. Are they professionals, amateurs, or student performers? Are they rehearsed and prepared for the performance? Are they cast appropriately for the role they are dancing? Look at the number of dancers on stage. Are there solo performers? Do they perform as a duo, or a pas de deux (step of two)? Are there both male and female dancers, and how do they interact?

The Lighting—Look at the colors of lighting that has been selected. Were "warm" tones, such as yellows or reds used, or were "cool" tones such as greens or blues selected? What lights were used (for example, spot lights, head lights, shin lights?)

Set/scenery—Describe the scenery. Was there a painted backdrop, or was a simple "cyc" that was lit used? What props, if any, were used? Describe the scenery in detail.

Costumes/Make-up—What type of costume was used? What colors and fabrics were selected? Is elaborate make-up used, or simple stage make-up for the dancers? Describe the types of shoes (if any) worn by the dancers.

Music—Is the music recorded, or is it being performed by live musicians or an orchestra? Is the music classical, or is it more discordant, or even computer generated? Consider how the music works with the choreography.

Overall impression—Did you enjoy the performance? Describe your reactions to the piece.

DANCE PERFORMANCE REVIEW

You are required to attend several dance concerts as a class requirement, because it is through the observation of live performances that you will begin to have an appreciation for dance. As you watch **each** piece within each performance, please use this form to answer the questions listed below. Answer every question about each dance that you watch, and turn in these reviews at the class immediately following the performance.

Choreography—Who is the choreographer of the piece? What style or genre of dance is being performed? What is the choreographer trying to accomplish? Is he or she telling a story, or is the dance simply abstract, with no story line? What patterns may be observed? Is the entire stage used, with movements to both stage left and right, and both upstage and downstage? Or do the dancers remain somewhat stationary, with little movement across the stage? Was the choreographer successful in engaging your attention and appreciation?

The Dancers—Observe the performance of the dancers themselves. Are they professionals, amateurs, or student performers? Are they rehearsed and prepared for the performance? Are they cast appropriately for the role they are dancing? Look at the number of dancers on stage. Are there solo performers? Do they perform as a duo, or a pas de deux (step of two)? Are there both male and female dancers, and how do they interact?

The Lighting—Look at the colors of lighting that has been selected. Were "warm" tones, such as yellows or reds used, or were "cool" tones such as greens or blues selected? What lights were used (for example, spot lights, head lights, shin lights?)

Set/scenery—Describe the scenery. Was there a painted backdrop, or was a simple "cyc" that was lit used? What props, if any, were used? Describe the scenery in detail.

Costumes/Make-up—What type of costume was used? What colors and fabrics were selected? Is elaborate make-up used, or simple stage make-up for the dancers? Describe the types of shoes (if any) worn by the dancers.

Music—Is the music recorded, or is it being performed by live musicians or an orchestra? Is the music classical, or is it more discordant, or even computer generated? Consider how the music works with the choreography.

Overall impression—Did you enjoy the performance? Describe your reactions to the piece.

DANCE PERFORMANCE REVIEW

You are required to attend several dance concerts as a class requirement, because it is through the observation of live performances that you will begin to have an appreciation for dance. As you watch **each** piece within each performance, please use this form to answer the questions listed below. Answer every question about each dance that you watch, and turn in these reviews at the class immediately following the performance.

Choreography—Who is the choreographer of the piece? What style or genre of dance is being performed? What is the choreographer trying to accomplish? Is he or she telling a story, or is the dance simply abstract, with no story line? What patterns may be observed? Is the entire stage used, with movements to both stage left and right, and both upstage and downstage? Or do the dancers remain somewhat stationary, with little movement across the stage? Was the choreographer successful in engaging your attention and appreciation?

The Dancers—Observe the performance of the dancers themselves. Are they professionals, amateurs, or student performers? Are they rehearsed and prepared for the performance? Are they cast appropriately for the role they are dancing? Look at the number of dancers on stage. Are there solo performers? Do they perform as a duo, or a pas de deux (step of two)? Are there both male and female dancers, and how do they interact?

The Lighting—Look at the colors of lighting that has been selected. Were "warm" tones, such as yellows or reds used, or were "cool" tones such as greens or blues selected? What lights were used (for example, spot lights, head lights, shin lights?)

Set/scenery—Describe the scenery. Was there a painted backdrop, or was a simple "cyc" that was lit used? What props, if any, were used? Describe the scenery in detail.

Costumes/Make-up—What type of costume was used? What colors and fabrics were selected? Is elaborate make-up used, or simple stage make-up for the dancers? Describe the types of shoes (if any) worn by the dancers.

Music—Is the music recorded, or is it being performed by live musicians or an orchestra? Is the music classical, or is it more discordant, or even computer generated? Consider how the music works with the choreography.

Overall impression—Did you enjoy the performance? Describe your reactions to the piece.

DANCE PERFORMANCE REVIEW

You are required to attend several dance concerts as a class requirement, because it is through the observation of live performances that you will begin to have an appreciation for dance. As you watch **each** piece within each performance, please use this form to answer the questions listed below. Answer every question about each dance that you watch, and turn in these reviews at the class immediately following the performance.

Choreography—Who is the choreographer of the piece? What style or genre of dance is being performed? What is the choreographer trying to accomplish? Is he or she telling a story, or is the dance simply abstract, with no story line? What patterns may be observed? Is the entire stage used, with movements to both stage left and right, and both upstage and downstage? Or do the dancers remain somewhat stationary, with little movement across the stage? Was the choreographer successful in engaging your attention and appreciation?

The Dancers—Observe the performance of the dancers themselves. Are they professionals, amateurs, or student performers? Are they rehearsed and prepared for the performance? Are they cast appropriately for the role they are dancing? Look at the number of dancers on stage. Are there solo performers? Do they perform as a duo, or a pas de deux (step of two)? Are there both male and female dancers, and how do they interact?

The Lighting—Look at the colors of lighting that has been selected. Were "warm" tones, such as yellows or reds used, or were "cool" tones such as greens or blues selected? What lights were used (for example, spot lights, head lights, shin lights?)

Set/scenery—Describe the scenery. Was there a painted backdrop, or was a simple "cyc" that was lit used? What props, if any, were used? Describe the scenery in detail.

Costumes/Make-up—What type of costume was used? What colors and fabrics were selected? Is elaborate make-up used, or simple stage make-up for the dancers? Describe the types of shoes (if any) worn by the dancers..

Music—Is the music recorded, or is it being performed by live musicians or an orchestra? Is the music classical, or is it more discordant, or even computer generated? Consider how the music works with the choreography.

Overall impression—Did you enjoy the performance? Describe your reactions to the piece.

DANCE PERFORMANCE REVIEW

You are required to attend several dance concerts as a class requirement, because it is through the observation of live performances that you will begin to have an appreciation for dance. As you watch **each** piece within each performance, please use this form to answer the questions listed below. Answer every question about each dance that you watch, and turn in these reviews at the class immediately following the performance.

Choreography—Who is the choreographer of the piece? What style or genre of dance is being performed? What is the choreographer trying to accomplish? Is he or she telling a story, or is the dance simply abstract, with no story line? What patterns may be observed? Is the entire stage used, with movements to both stage left and right, and both upstage and downstage? Or do the dancers remain somewhat stationary, with little movement across the stage? Was the choreographer successful in engaging your attention and appreciation?

The Dancers—Observe the performance of the dancers themselves. Are they professionals, amateurs, or student performers? Are they rehearsed and prepared for the performance? Are they cast appropriately for the role they are dancing? Look at the number of dancers on stage. Are there solo performers? Do they perform as a duo, or a pas de deux (step of two)? Are there both male and female dancers, and how do they interact?

The Lighting—Look at the colors of lighting that has been selected. Were "warm" tones, such as yellows or reds used, or were "cool" tones such as greens or blues selected? What lights were used (for example, spot lights, head lights, shin lights?)

Set/scenery—Describe the scenery. Was there a painted backdrop, or was a simple "cyc" that was lit used? What props, if any, were used? Describe the scenery in detail.

Costumes/Make-up—What type of costume was used? What colors and fabrics were selected? Is elaborate make-up used, or simple stage make-up for the dancers? Describe the types of shoes (if any) worn by the dancers.

Music—Is the music recorded, or is it being performed by live musicians or an orchestra? Is the music classical, or is it more discordant, or even computer generated? Consider how the music works with the choreography.

Overall impression—Did you enjoy the performance? Describe your reactions to the piece.

DANCE PERFORMANCE REVIEW

You are required to attend several dance concerts as a class requirement, because it is through the observation of live performances that you will begin to have an appreciation for dance. As you watch **each** piece within each performance, please use this form to answer the questions listed below. Answer every question about each dance that you watch, and turn in these reviews at the class immediately following the performance.

Choreography—Who is the choreographer of the piece? What style or genre of dance is being performed? What is the choreographer trying to accomplish? Is he or she telling a story, or is the dance simply abstract, with no story line? What patterns may be observed? Is the entire stage used, with movements to both stage left and right, and both upstage and downstage? Or do the dancers remain somewhat stationary, with little movement across the stage? Was the choreographer successful in engaging your attention and appreciation?

The Dancers—Observe the performance of the dancers themselves. Are they professionals, amateurs, or student performers? Are they rehearsed and prepared for the performance? Are they cast appropriately for the role they are dancing? Look at the number of dancers on stage. Are there solo performers? Do they perform as a duo, or a pas de deux (step of two)? Are there both male and female dancers, and how do they interact?

The Lighting—Look at the colors of lighting that has been selected. Were "warm" tones, such as yellows or reds used, or were "cool" tones such as greens or blues selected? What lights were used (for example, spot lights, head lights, shin lights?)

Set/scenery—Describe the scenery. Was there a painted backdrop, or was a simple "cyc" that was lit used? What props, if any, were used? Describe the scenery in detail.

Costumes/Make-up—What type of costume was used? What colors and fabrics were selected? Is elaborate make-up used, or simple stage make-up for the dancers? Describe the types of shoes (if any) worn by the dancers.

Music—Is the music recorded, or is it being performed by live musicians or an orchestra? Is the music classical, or is it more discordant, or even computer generated? Consider how the music works with the choreography.

Overall impression—Did you enjoy the performance? Describe your reactions to the piece.

DANCE PERFORMANCE REVIEW

You are required to attend several dance concerts as a class requirement, because it is through the observation of live performances that you will begin to have an appreciation for dance. As you watch **each** piece within each performance, please use this form to answer the questions listed below. Answer every question about each dance that you watch, and turn in these reviews at the class immediately following the performance.

Choreography—Who is the choreographer of the piece? What style or genre of dance is being performed? What is the choreographer trying to accomplish? Is he or she telling a story, or is the dance simply abstract, with no story line? What patterns may be observed? Is the entire stage used, with movements to both stage left and right, and both upstage and downstage? Or do the dancers remain somewhat stationary, with little movement across the stage? Was the choreographer successful in engaging your attention and appreciation?

The Dancers—Observe the performance of the dancers themselves. Are they professionals, amateurs, or student performers? Are they rehearsed and prepared for the performance? Are they cast appropriately for the role they are dancing? Look at the number of dancers on stage. Are there solo performers? Do they perform as a duo, or a pas de deux (step of two)? Are there both male and female dancers, and how do they interact?

The Lighting—Look at the colors of lighting that has been selected. Were "warm" tones, such as yellows or reds used, or were "cool" tones such as greens or blues selected? What lights were used (for example, spot lights, head lights, shin lights?)

Set/scenery—Describe the scenery. Was there a painted backdrop, or was a simple "cyc" that was lit used? What props, if any, were used? Describe the scenery in detail.

Costumes/Make-up—What type of costume was used? What colors and fabrics were selected? Is elaborate make-up used, or simple stage make-up for the dancers? Describe the types of shoes (if any) worn by the dancers.

Music—Is the music recorded, or is it being performed by live musicians or an orchestra? Is the music classical, or is it more discordant, or even computer generated? Consider how the music works with the choreography.

Overall impression—Did you enjoy the performance? Describe your reactions to the piece.

DANCE PERFORMANCE REVIEW

You are required to attend several dance concerts as a class requirement, because it is through the observation of live performances that you will begin to have an appreciation for dance. As you watch **each** piece within each performance, please use this form to answer the questions listed below. Answer every question about each dance that you watch, and turn in these reviews at the class immediately following the performance.

Choreography—Who is the choreographer of the piece? What style or genre of dance is being performed? What is the choreographer trying to accomplish? Is he or she telling a story, or is the dance simply abstract, with no story line? What patterns may be observed? Is the entire stage used, with movements to both stage left and right, and both upstage and downstage? Or do the dancers remain somewhat stationary, with little movement across the stage? Was the choreographer successful in engaging your attention and appreciation?

The Dancers—Observe the performance of the dancers themselves. Are they professionals, amateurs, or student performers? Are they rehearsed and prepared for the performance? Are they cast appropriately for the role they are dancing? Look at the number of dancers on stage. Are there solo performers? Do they perform as a duo, or a pas de deux (step of two)? Are there both male and female dancers, and how do they interact?

The Lighting—Look at the colors of lighting that has been selected. Were "warm" tones, such as yellows or reds used, or were "cool" tones such as greens or blues selected? What lights were used (for example, spot lights, head lights, shin lights?)

Set/scenery—Describe the scenery. Was there a painted backdrop, or was a simple "cyc" that was lit used? What props, if any, were used? Describe the scenery in detail.

Costumes/Make-up—What type of costume was used? What colors and fabrics were selected? Is elaborate make-up used, or simple stage make-up for the dancers? Describe the types of shoes (if any) worn by the dancers.

Music—Is the music recorded, or is it being performed by live musicians or an orchestra? Is the music classical, or is it more discordant, or even computer generated? Consider how the music works with the choreography.

Overall impression—Did you enjoy the performance? Describe your reactions to the piece.

DANCE PERFORMANCE REVIEW

You are required to attend several dance concerts as a class requirement, because it is through the observation of live performances that you will begin to have an appreciation for dance. As you watch **each** piece within each performance, please use this form to answer the questions listed below. Answer every question about each dance that you watch, and turn in these reviews at the class immediately following the performance.

Choreography—Who is the choreographer of the piece? What style or genre of dance is being performed? What is the choreographer trying to accomplish? Is he or she telling a story, or is the dance simply abstract, with no story line? What patterns may be observed? Is the entire stage used, with movements to both stage left and right, and both upstage and downstage? Or do the dancers remain somewhat stationary, with little movement across the stage? Was the choreographer successful in engaging your attention and appreciation?

The Dancers—Observe the performance of the dancers themselves. Are they professionals, amateurs, or student performers? Are they rehearsed and prepared for the performance? Are they cast appropriately for the role they are dancing? Look at the number of dancers on stage. Are there solo performers? Do they perform as a duo, or a pas de deux (step of two)? Are there both male and female dancers, and how do they interact?

The Lighting—Look at the colors of lighting that has been selected. Were "warm" tones, such as yellows or reds used, or were "cool" tones such as greens or blues selected? What lights were used (for example, spot lights, head lights, shin lights?)

Set/scenery—Describe the scenery. Was there a painted backdrop, or was a simple "cyc" that was lit used? What props, if any, were used? Describe the scenery in detail.

Costumes/Make-up—What type of costume was used? What colors and fabrics were selected? Is elaborate make-up used, or simple stage make-up for the dancers? Describe the types of shoes (if any) worn by the dancers.

Music—Is the music recorded, or is it being performed by live musicians or an orchestra? Is the music classical, or is it more discordant, or even computer generated? Consider how the music works with the choreography.

Overall impression—Did you enjoy the performance? Describe your reactions to the piece.

DANCE PERFORMANCE REVIEW

You are required to attend several dance concerts as a class requirement, because it is through the observation of live performances that you will begin to have an appreciation for dance. As you watch **each** piece within each performance, please use this form to answer the questions listed below. Answer every question about each dance that you watch, and turn in these reviews at the class immediately following the performance.

Choreography—Who is the choreographer of the piece? What style or genre of dance is being performed? What is the choreographer trying to accomplish? Is he or she telling a story, or is the dance simply abstract, with no story line? What patterns may be observed? Is the entire stage used, with movements to both stage left and right, and both upstage and downstage? Or do the dancers remain somewhat stationary, with little movement across the stage? Was the choreographer successful in engaging your attention and appreciation?

The Dancers—Observe the performance of the dancers themselves. Are they professionals, amateurs, or student performers? Are they rehearsed and prepared for the performance? Are they cast appropriately for the role they are dancing? Look at the number of dancers on stage. Are there solo performers? Do they perform as a duo, or a pas de deux (step of two)? Are there both male and female dancers, and how do they interact?

The Lighting—Look at the colors of lighting that has been selected. Were "warm" tones, such as yellows or reds used, or were "cool" tones such as greens or blues selected? What lights were used (for example, spot lights, head lights, shin lights?)

137

Set/scenery—Describe the scenery. Was there a painted backdrop, or was a simple "cyc" that was lit used? What props, if any, were used? Describe the scenery in detail.

Costumes/Make-up—What type of costume was used? What colors and fabrics were selected? Is elaborate make-up used, or simple stage make-up for the dancers? Describe the types of shoes (if any) worn by the dancers.

Music—Is the music recorded, or is it being performed by live musicians or an orchestra? Is the music classical, or is it more discordant, or even computer generated? Consider how the music works with the choreography.

Overall impression—Did you enjoy the performance? Describe your reactions to the piece.

DANCE PERFORMANCE REVIEW

You are required to attend several dance concerts as a class requirement, because it is through the observation of live performances that you will begin to have an appreciation for dance. As you watch **each** piece within each performance, please use this form to answer the questions listed below. Answer every question about each dance that you watch, and turn in these reviews at the class immediately following the performance.

Choreography—Who is the choreographer of the piece? What style or genre of dance is being performed? What is the choreographer trying to accomplish? Is he or she telling a story, or is the dance simply abstract, with no story line? What patterns may be observed? Is the entire stage used, with movements to both stage left and right, and both upstage and downstage? Or do the dancers remain somewhat stationary, with little movement across the stage? Was the choreographer successful in engaging your attention and appreciation?

The Dancers—Observe the performance of the dancers themselves. Are they professionals, amateurs, or student performers? Are they rehearsed and prepared for the performance? Are they cast appropriately for the role they are dancing? Look at the number of dancers on stage. Are there solo performers? Do they perform as a duo, or a pas de deux (step of two)? Are there both male and female dancers, and how do they interact?

The Lighting—Look at the colors of lighting that has been selected. Were "warm" tones, such as yellows or reds used, or were "cool" tones such as greens or blues selected? What lights were used (for example, spot lights, head lights, shin lights?)

Set/scenery—Describe the scenery. Was there a painted backdrop, or was a simple "cyc" that was lit used? What props, if any, were used? Describe the scenery in detail.

Costumes/Make-up—What type of costume was used? What colors and fabrics were selected? Is elaborate make-up used, or simple stage make-up for the dancers? Describe the types of shoes (if any) worn by the dancers.

Music—Is the music recorded, or is it being performed by live musicians or an orchestra? Is the music classical, or is it more discordant, or even computer generated? Consider how the music works with the choreography.

Overall impression—Did you enjoy the performance? Describe your reactions to the piece.

DANCE PERFORMANCE REVIEW

You are required to attend several dance concerts as a class requirement, because it is through the observation of live performances that you will begin to have an appreciation for dance. As you watch **each** piece within each performance, please use this form to answer the questions listed below. Answer every question about each dance that you watch, and turn in these reviews at the class immediately following the performance.

Choreography—Who is the choreographer of the piece? What style or genre of dance is being performed? What is the choreographer trying to accomplish? Is he or she telling a story, or is the dance simply abstract, with no story line? What patterns may be observed? Is the entire stage used, with movements to both stage left and right, and both upstage and downstage? Or do the dancers remain somewhat stationary, with little movement across the stage? Was the choreographer successful in engaging your attention and appreciation?

The Dancers—Observe the performance of the dancers themselves. Are they professionals, amateurs, or student performers? Are they rehearsed and prepared for the performance? Are they cast appropriately for the role they are dancing? Look at the number of dancers on stage. Are there solo performers? Do they perform as a duo, or a pas de deux (step of two)? Are there both male and female dancers, and how do they interact?

The Lighting—Look at the colors of lighting that has been selected. Were "warm" tones, such as yellows or reds used, or were "cool" tones such as greens or blues selected? What lights were used (for example, spot lights, head lights, shin lights?)

Set/scenery—Describe the scenery. Was there a painted backdrop, or was a simple "cyc" that was lit used? What props, if any, were used? Describe the scenery in detail.

Costumes/Make-up—What type of costume was used? What colors and fabrics were selected? Is elaborate make-up used, or simple stage make-up for the dancers? Describe the types of shoes (if any) worn by the dancers.

Music—Is the music recorded, or is it being performed by live musicians or an orchestra? Is the music classical, or is it more discordant, or even computer generated? Consider how the music works with the choreography.

Overall impression—Did you enjoy the performance? Describe your reactions to the piece.

DANCE PERFORMANCE REVIEW

You are required to attend several dance concerts as a class requirement, because it is through the observation of live performances that you will begin to have an appreciation for dance. As you watch **each** piece within each performance, please use this form to answer the questions listed below. Answer every question about each dance that you watch, and turn in these reviews at the class immediately following the performance.

Choreography—Who is the choreographer of the piece? What style or genre of dance is being performed? What is the choreographer trying to accomplish? Is he or she telling a story, or is the dance simply abstract, with no story line? What patterns may be observed? Is the entire stage used, with movements to both stage left and right, and both upstage and downstage? Or do the dancers remain somewhat stationary, with little movement across the stage? Was the choreographer successful in engaging your attention and appreciation?

The Dancers—Observe the performance of the dancers themselves. Are they professionals, amateurs, or student performers? Are they rehearsed and prepared for the performance? Are they cast appropriately for the role they are dancing? Look at the number of dancers on stage. Are there solo performers? Do they perform as a duo, or a pas de deux (step of two)? Are there both male and female dancers, and how do they interact?

The Lighting—Look at the colors of lighting that has been selected. Were "warm" tones, such as yellows or reds used, or were "cool" tones such as greens or blues selected? What lights were used (for example, spot lights, head lights, shin lights?)

Set/scenery—Describe the scenery. Was there a painted backdrop, or was a simple "cyc" that was lit used? What props, if any, were used? Describe the scenery in detail.

Costumes/Make-up—What type of costume was used? What colors and fabrics were selected? Is elaborate make-up used, or simple stage make-up for the dancers? Describe the types of shoes (if any) worn by the dancers.

Music—Is the music recorded, or is it being performed by live musicians or an orchestra? Is the music classical, or is it more discordant, or even computer generated? Consider how the music works with the choreography.

Overall impression—Did you enjoy the performance? Describe your reactions to the piece.

DANCE PERFORMANCE REVIEW

You are required to attend several dance concerts as a class requirement, because it is through the observation of live performances that you will begin to have an appreciation for dance. As you watch **each** piece within each performance, please use this form to answer the questions listed below. Answer every question about each dance that you watch, and turn in these reviews at the class immediately following the performance.

Choreography—Who is the choreographer of the piece? What style or genre of dance is being performed? What is the choreographer trying to accomplish? Is he or she telling a story, or is the dance simply abstract, with no story line? What patterns may be observed? Is the entire stage used, with movements to both stage left and right, and both upstage and downstage? Or do the dancers remain somewhat stationary, with little movement across the stage? Was the choreographer successful in engaging your attention and appreciation?

The Dancers—Observe the performance of the dancers themselves. Are they professionals, amateurs, or student performers? Are they rehearsed and prepared for the performance? Are they cast appropriately for the role they are dancing? Look at the number of dancers on stage. Are there solo performers? Do they perform as a duo, or a pas de deux (step of two)? Are there both male and female dancers, and how do they interact?

The Lighting—Look at the colors of lighting that has been selected. Were "warm" tones, such as yellows or reds used, or were "cool" tones such as greens or blues selected? What lights were used (for example, spot lights, head lights, shin lights?)

Set/scenery—Describe the scenery. Was there a painted backdrop, or was a simple "cyc" that was lit used? What props, if any, were used? Describe the scenery in detail.

Costumes/Make-up—What type of costume was used? What colors and fabrics were selected? Is elaborate make-up used, or simple stage make-up for the dancers? Describe the types of shoes (if any) worn by the dancers.

Music—Is the music recorded, or is it being performed by live musicians or an orchestra? Is the music classical, or is it more discordant, or even computer generated? Consider how the music works with the choreography.

Overall impression—Did you enjoy the performance? Describe your reactions to the piece.

DANCE PERFORMANCE REVIEW

You are required to attend several dance concerts as a class requirement, because it is through the observation of live performances that you will begin to have an appreciation for dance. As you watch **each** piece within each performance, please use this form to answer the questions listed below. Answer every question about each dance that you watch, and turn in these reviews at the class immediately following the performance.

Choreography—Who is the choreographer of the piece? What style or genre of dance is being performed? What is the choreographer trying to accomplish? Is he or she telling a story, or is the dance simply abstract, with no story line? What patterns may be observed? Is the entire stage used, with movements to both stage left and right, and both upstage and downstage? Or do the dancers remain somewhat stationary, with little movement across the stage? Was the choreographer successful in engaging your attention and appreciation?

The Dancers—Observe the performance of the dancers themselves. Are they professionals, amateurs, or student performers? Are they rehearsed and prepared for the performance? Are they cast appropriately for the role they are dancing? Look at the number of dancers on stage. Are there solo performers? Do they perform as a duo, or a pas de deux (step of two)? Are there both male and female dancers, and how do they interact?

The Lighting—Look at the colors of lighting that has been selected. Were "warm" tones, such as yellows or reds used, or were "cool" tones such as greens or blues selected? What lights were used (for example, spot lights, head lights, shin lights?)

Set/scenery—Describe the scenery. Was there a painted backdrop, or was a simple "cyc" that was lit used? What props, if any, were used? Describe the scenery in detail.

Costumes/Make-up—What type of costume was used? What colors and fabrics were selected? Is elaborate make-up used, or simple stage make-up for the dancers? Describe the types of shoes (if any) worn by the dancers.

Music—Is the music recorded, or is it being performed by live musicians or an orchestra? Is the music classical, or is it more discordant, or even computer generated? Consider how the music works with the choreography.

Overall impression—Did you enjoy the performance? Describe your reactions to the piece.

VISITING PERFORMER EVALUATION

As often as possible, guest performers will demonstrate dance technique to the class. Ballet, modern, hip hop, tap, step dancing, ballroom and other social dancing will be introduced. Please use this form to evaluate the guest artists.

What are the guest artists' names, and what type or genre of dance are they demonstrating?

Describe what type of costume, including shoes, that they wore.

What type of training and classes have these performers undertaken?

What type of music, if any, was used?

Describe the dance/demonstration.

VISITING PERFORMER EVALUATION

As often as possible, guest performers will demonstrate dance technique to the class. Ballet, modern, hip hop, tap, step dancing, ballroom and other social dancing will be introduced. Please use this form to evaluate the guest artists.

What are the guest artists' names, and what type or genre of dance are they demonstrating?

Describe what type of costume, including shoes, that they wore.

What type of training and classes have these performers undertaken?

What type of music, if any, was used?

Describe the dance/demonstration.

VISITING PERFORMER EVALUATION

As often as possible, guest performers will demonstrate dance technique to the class. Ballet, modern, hip hop, tap, step dancing, ballroom and other social dancing will be introduced. Please use this form to evaluate the guest artists.

What are the guest artists' names, and what type or genre of dance are they demonstrating?

Describe what type of costume, including shoes, that they wore.

What type of training and classes have these performers undertaken?

What type of music, if any, was used?

Describe the dance/demonstration.

VISITING PERFORMER EVALUATION

As often as possible, guest performers will demonstrate dance technique to the class. Ballet, modern, hip hop, tap, step dancing, ballroom and other social dancing will be introduced. Please use this form to evaluate the guest artists.

What are the guest artists' names, and what type or genre of dance are they demonstrating?

Describe what type of costume, including shoes, that they wore.

What type of training and classes have these performers undertaken?

What type of music, if any, was used?

Describe the dance/demonstration.

VISITING PERFORMER EVALUATION

As often as possible, guest performers will demonstrate dance technique to the class. Ballet, modern, hip hop, tap, step dancing, ballroom and other social dancing will be introduced. Please use this form to evaluate the guest artists.

What are the guest artists' names, and what type or genre of dance are they demonstrating?

Describe what type of costume, including shoes, that they wore.

What type of training and classes have these performers undertaken?

What type of music, if any, was used?

Describe the dance/demonstration.

VISITING PERFORMER EVALUATION

As often as possible, guest performers will demonstrate dance technique to the class. Ballet, modern, hip hop, tap, step dancing, ballroom and other social dancing will be introduced. Please use this form to evaluate the guest artists.

What are the guest artists' names, and what type or genre of dance are they demonstrating?

Describe what type of costume, including shoes, that they wore.

What type of training and classes have these performers undertaken?

What type of music, if any, was used?

Describe the dance/demonstration.